Truth as Encounter

BOOKS BY
EMIL BRUNNER
Published by The Westminster Press
®

Truth as Encounter, A New Edition, Much Enlarged, of "The Divine-Human Encounter"
(*Wahrheit als Begegnung*)

The Christian Doctrine of the Church, Faith, and the Consummation, Dogmatics: Vol. III
(*Die christliche Lehre von der Kirche, vom Glauben, und von der Vollendung*)

I Believe in the Living God
(*Ich glaube an den lebendigen Gott*)

The Letter to the Romans
(*Der Römerbrief*)

Faith, Hope, and Love

The Great Invitation, and Other Sermons
(*Fraumünster-Predigten*)

Eternal Hope
(*Das Ewige als Zukunft und Gegenwart*)

The Misunderstanding of the Church
(*Das Missverständnis der Kirche*)

The Christian Doctrine of Creation and Redemption, Dogmatics: Vol. II
(*Die christliche Lehre von Schöpfung und Erlösung*)

The Scandal of Christianity

The Christian Doctrine of God, Dogmatics: Vol. I
(*Die christliche Lehre von Gott*)

Man in Revolt
(*Der Mensch im Widerspruch*)

The Mediator
(*Der Mittler*)

The Divine Imperative
(*Das Gebot und die Ordnungen*)

Revelation and Reason
(*Offenbarung und Vernunft*)

TRUTH
AS
ENCOUNTER

by
Emil Brunner

A New Edition, Much Enlarged,
of The Divine-Human Encounter

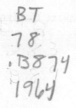

BT
78
.B874
1964

THE WESTMINSTER PRESS
Philadelphia

This book was published originally in German as *Wahrheit als
Begegnung,* © Zwingli-Verlag, Zurich, 1938, and first published
in English as *The Divine-Human Encounter* in 1943. The present volume is a translation of the second edition, 1963, of
Wahrheit als Begegnung, enlarged with a new " Part One." The
English translation of the first edition was prepared by Aman-
dus W. Loos. The translator of the new part and the corrections
of the original English text were prepared by David Cairns in
consultation with T. H. L. Parker.

LIBRARY OF CONGRESS CATALOG CARD No. 64–11192

PUBLISHED BY THE WESTMINSTER PRESS®
PHILADELPHIA, PENNSYLVANIA 19107

PRINTED IN THE UNITED STATES OF AMERICA

Contents

xi

Preface to the English Translation
of the Second Edition

THIS BOOK, which first appeared in English translation in 1943, bore, through the caprice of the translator and the publisher, the title *The Divine-Human Encounter*, although in the original it was called *Truth as Encounter*. Under this title, which eliminated or at least very much weakened the paradox of the original title, it has made its way, and has become known in the English-speaking world. The publisher can thus justify his caprice by referring to its success, and I grant him retrospectively the absolution for which he had never asked.

But now the time has come when the book must appear with its original, confessedly paradoxical title, from which it will for the first time become clear that the *truth* as the Bible understands this word is its theme. What at that time, in 1943, might have been a risk may well in the interval have become the opposite: an attraction. The paradox is not just thrown down before the reader as something unintelligible; it is copiously explained and substantiated, as can be seen from the general Introduction to this second edition. I hope that the reader will be grateful for this decision.

EMIL BRUNNER

Zurich, January, 1963

1

Foreword to the First Edition

THIS INQUIRY into the Christian understanding of truth is a series of lectures, in part considerably revised, which were delivered on the Olaus Petri Foundation at the University of Uppsala in the fall of 1937. The suggestion to make the relation between the objective and the subjective in Christian faith the theme of the lectures was given by my friend, Prof. A. Runestam, of Uppsala, at that time the president of the Foundation. This theme has proved to be an extremely valuable starting point for reflection about the Biblical concept of truth — reflection which led to the insight, important alike for theology and the practical work of the church, that our understanding of the message of salvation and also of the church's task is still burdened with the subject-object antithesis, which originated in Greek philosophy. The Biblical conception of truth is: truth as encounter. Applying this knowledge in all spheres of church doctrine and practice is of quite incalculable import; in this application I am aware that I have made only a modest beginning. But surely I may hope that this first advance will be of interest to all who take seriously the Reformation interpretation of Scripture. If my thesis in these lectures really represents faithfully the Biblical understanding of truth, then indeed much of our thinking and action in the church must be different from what we have been accustomed to for centuries.

Since I am convinced of the fallibility of the theological teacher — whoever he may be — I lay these results before my fellow searchers for criticism. But I trust that they will agree with the main points, at least insofar as the Bible itself, and not some specific dogma about it, is the final authority.

E. B.

Zurich, March, 1938

2

Foreword to the Second Edition

THE FUNDAMENTAL IDEA of this book, which is formulated in the title, *Truth as Encounter*, came to me as I was meditating on the theme of my Olaus Petri Lectures, " Objectivism and Subjectivism in Theology and the Church," which had been suggested to me by Prof. A. Runestam, the president of the Foundation at that time. I soon saw that it could only be formulated " beyond objectivism and subjectivism," and the concept of " Truth as Encounter " came intuitively to my mind as the overcoming of this antithesis.

These lectures were delivered by me in 1937 in Uppsala, and published in German in 1938, and I have set forth the significance of their fundamental idea for theology and the church in my subsequent works, *Revelation and Reason*, and the three volumes of my *Dogmatics*, the last of which was published as recently as 1960 [in English, 1962]. On the other hand, I have never set it in its place within the context of the general philosophical problem of truth. This omission was justified, inasmuch as only thus could the very natural misconception be avoided that here I was expounding a philosophy cut adrift from, or even presupposed by, the Christian faith; in fact, that I was doing something like what Schleiermacher did in the imposing Introduction to his book *The Christian Faith*, where by borrowing basic " Propositions " from the " Dialectic " and the philosophical " Ethics " he dovetailed his Dogmatics into a philosophy independent of faith, and preceding it in order of presentation. The theme of these lectures of mine, and its development in the above-named theological works, made it clear that such a subordination of theology to philosophy was unthinkable. On the other hand, my restraint, of which I have spoken, had the result that only a comparatively small number of people

3

realized the significance of the Christian understanding of truth formulated in the title for the problem of truth in general.

The aim of this Introduction is now to make good this earlier omission and to expound and defend the Christian concept of truth in its antithesis to the naturalistic-positivistic and idealistic-speculative concepts. At the same time I shall be illustrating by a concrete example what I later postulated in *Revelation and Reason* [1941; E.T., 1946] as Christian philosophy. I am convinced that what is here understood as truth has its origin in the New Testament witness to Christ as it is expressed in the Prologue to John's Gospel, "Grace and truth came by Jesus Christ" (John 1: 17). Truth that has come into being, or come — for the thinker an unintelligible or even nonsensical juxtaposition — it is precisely this paradox which it is the purpose of John's Gospel to attest. That which philosophy or mysticism conceives of as the essential timeless, transcendent ground of being is here described as a happening. The transcendent ground of truth moves from a hidden transcendence into history. Here we have to do with a happening in which the truth that is identical with grace discloses itself to man and bestows itself upon him. That the Ground of all being should come to man, and not be found by him, this is what the Gospel tells us, and in so doing, it expresses the difference between the Biblical understanding of truth and all others. The detailed examination of this theme is the aim of this book, and the purpose of the new "Part One" is to make clear the contrast between this understanding of truth and all other concepts of truth.

I am grateful to the Zwingli-Verlag for its decision to publish a new edition of this study, which is of basic importance to my whole theological work. The preparation of the introductory part and the republication of the earlier book was possible for me only through the loyal cooperation of Frau Dr. Guanella-Zietzschmann, to whom I express also at this point my heartiest thanks for her great help.

E. B.

Zurich, January, 1963

PART ONE

Introduction:
The Christian Understanding of Truth
in Relation to the Philosophico–Scientific
Understanding

I

Idealism
and Naturalism

T RUTH AS ENCOUNTER " is a concept of truth unknown to
philosophy and science. In this book it receives its first expression and systematic formulation. The whole of Western
philosophy and the science that has issued from it are dominated
by the object-subject antithesis. Expressed in the categories of
ancient Greece, this was at first the antithesis of *physis* and
idea, and only since the Renaissance and the Reformation was
it sharpened into the antithesis of object and subject. After
several centuries of tentative speculations in natural philosophy,
Greek philosophy found its theme with Socrates and Plato, the
truth about man. Physics, the Platonic Socrates [1] tells us, is not
the concern of man. The authentic theme of philosophy is the
inquiry about man. But this truth, says Socrates, the philosopher
cannot and must not teach. Even if only latent, it is already *in*
every man. The philosopher has only the humble " midwife's
task " to perform, by bringing it to light. This is the Greek, the
idealistic, idea of truth, as it is already contained in the word
a-lētheia.[2] In it the concept of the a priori idea is implicit.

[1] " That physics is not the concern of men." Plato, quoted from
Diogenes Laertius, II. v. 21, in Kierkegaard, *Philosophical Fragments*, p. 7.
[2] TWNT I, p. 239: " *Alētheia* — etymologically ' nonconceal-
ment ' or ' concealment of nothing ' — means originally a fact or
state of affairs insofar as it is seen, shown, or expressed, and in such
seeing, showing, or speech is fully disclosed or discloses itself as it
really is, bearing in mind the possibility that it could also be concealed, misrepresented, distorted, or suppressed. Thus *alētheia* is the

7

This has a twofold origin — in mathematics and in ethics. In mathematics — more precisely, in geometry — it had already dawned on Plato that the pure, perfect geometrical figures, for example, the straight line or the circle or the triangle, can never be found in the experiential world of sense perception, that they do not enter into us from without by instruction, but are present as a (latent) possession in our mind.[3] Thus they are not apprehended by the senses, but by thinking, and are to be " seen " as " thought-things " (*nooumena*); " idea " comes from *idein*, " to see." No one has ever yet seen a perfect circle. Only the " intellectual eye " of *nous* sees it, and everyone who is capable of thought sees this " thought-thing," and sees it in the same manner. And thus the whole world of sense perception turns out to be an " impure " copy of the ideas, which are the perfect original images, free from all accidental impurity. Nor can these ideas be gained by abstraction, i.e., through disregard of the accidents and imperfections of what is given to the senses, or through " purification " or intensification of the knowledge of the senses, since in order to purify it or raise it to a higher power, we would have already to know what to disregard and in which direction to intensify. The measure, the model, the idea itself, must therefore already be implicit in us, and cannot be introduced into us from outside of us.

But what holds good in mathematics holds good also in knowledge about the good, about " virtue," which was the primary interest of the Platonic Socrates. Knowledge about the true good is also not to be won from sense experience. This, too, from the very beginning, is implicit *in* us. It can only be seen by the eye of the mind. So if we inquire about the truth about man or about the true man, the answer is clear: the true man is the man as he is seen in the idea, the man of the world of ideas. He is at the same time the immortal, the eternal man. Thus life is

---

full or ' actual ' state of affairs . . . , and so its most frequently used contraries are *pseudos* (deception) and *doxa* (appearance, mere opinion), which conceal or distort *alētheia* . . . and in philosophy the question arises whether truth is grasped or not grasped."

[3] Cf. especially Plato's Dialogue *Meno*.

8

true only in proportion as it participates in this ideal, is like it, or approximates it. Through this thought of the ethical ideal, idealism has exercised its most powerful influence in the history of mankind, while the a priori nature of the idea was most clearly recognizable in mathematics. The ideal was at the same time the divine, since the idea of the good is the idea of ideas. Infinitely exalted above all that can be grasped by the senses, stands the ideal, the world of ideas.

In its later development, this antithesis between the world of the senses and the world of ideas was expanded into a metaphysic of mind. Mind is the true reality; mind is, above all, the knowing subject, the thinking self. Only through the positing of the thinking self do objects exist; only for the mind that knows is there an infinite cosmos. Truth is not *fact*, but mental act, *Tathandlung* (Fichte). *This* is the fundamental concept of the idealism of modern times, which imposes itself upon thought with the self-evidence of incontrovertibility, whereas empiricism had continually to suffer the reproach of being described as "naïve realism," as a standpoint that really only unreflecting men could be content to hold. On this thought rests the enthusiastic self-confidence of idealism.

But this self-confidence has not been able to withstand the criticism of the realists, although it has never been possible to refute idealism. Realism, whether naïve or not, has simply carried the day. Its triumph was principally due to the magnificent development of the natural sciences. Under their impact there came into being the so-called "positivistic" philosophy identical with naturalism, which brusquely bypasses the "speculations" of idealism, identifies truth with what is actually present to the senses, and dismisses every excursion or even inquiry that transcends the establishment of actual given fact, as fruitless trifling. Its "history of philosophy" consists of the simple assertion that we have passed from the childish era of religion and myth, and the adolescent era of metaphysic and speculation, into the adult era of the positive sciences. (A. Comte.) Thus it comes to the identification of truth and scientific knowledge as knowledge of what is actually present to the senses. But

9

this conception brought with it the relativization of the concept of truth.

It cannot be denied that man is, *among other things*, an object of knowledge, an object present to the senses, an object for the investigations of physics, chemistry, and biology. He, too, is a species of living creature, for which zoology finds a place in the morphological classification of the Linnaean system, and whose primitive forms have their place allocated to them within the evolution of life by the palaeanthropological department of palaeontology. It therefore follows that man is also the object of physiological psychology, and of that sociology which is defined by Auguste Comte, its creator, as " the physics of group-formation." The peculiarity of the positivistic conception of truth is not that it considers man, like every other entity, as an object given to the senses but, rather, that it believes itself able to grasp man *in his totality* thus, as an object. Its epistemological error is that it does not recognize the limits of this conception of man. This error was fated to have the most tragic consequences for the history of mankind.

Man as a perceptible object in the cosmos is a wholly insignificant, infinitesimal entity; he is, so to speak, a mere nothing in the processes of nature. The man who understands himself in terms of the physical universe, who considers himself wholly as a product of evolution, can no longer discover any meaning or value in this life of his. Everything that the faith of earlier times thought about God, freedom, and responsibility, everything that we are accustomed to include within the concept of human nature — man's creative power, the dignity of man, mind and culture, conscience, and so on — has no place left in the cosmos of the giant telescopes and the electron microscopes, but belongs to the world of childish or poetic mythology. Not only the " dear God " who cares as Provider and Father for his human children, but also duty and guilt, ideals and the striving for something higher, are products of myth-creating fantasy, about whose origin in the vital urge and life anxiety, and in the creation of emotive images, modern scientific psychology informs us. To wish to identify man with this partial aspect of

10

what is presented to the senses is to lose everything that is human.

If science, with the objectivism of its concept of truth, is *the* truth, then not only has the Christian faith no claim to truth, but the same is true of the Platonic world of ideas and of the world of Aristotle, which is permeated with the principle of entelechy, and of the logos of Heraclitus, which pervades the universe, not to mention the systems of the Middle Ages, ingeniously constructed by syntheses of ancient metaphysics with Christian faith, and the *harmonice mundi* of a Kepler, the theodicy of a Leibniz, and the splendid philosophies of the spirit of the German idealists — of Fichte, Schelling, and Hegel — which are all unraveled as fabrics of anthropomorphic mind-spinning. There is no place beside the celestial mechanics of Newton and the equally exact mechanics of modern genetics, biochemistry, and physiology for either Christian faith, understood as the truth about man, or for any mind metaphysics of idealistic thinkers. They may elevate us through their beauty or their profundity, but they are not true; they are illusion. This is what we are being told today, not only by the scientists themselves, but also by the realistic pictures of men and " reality " given to us by the poets who have had their illusions dispelled by the scientists.

Yes, it is so; a new age has come upon us, we must admit it, a hard, unfeeling, and cold reality in our world, which inexorably marches on over the wishes and dreams of our hearts, mercilessly treading down the idylls of earlier times. We must come to terms with it. We will attempt to master it, so far as, thanks to our scientific techniques, it is possible to do so. The electric brain, the imitation of the natural brain created and perfected by science, will here render us good, indispensable service. The instinct of self-preservation, which we share with all living things, together with the intelligence which distinguishes us from all other living creatures, and which has brought this new time upon us, will also allow us to master the problems of the life of society *without* the hitherto necessary props of religion, *without* the phrases about human dignity and reverence for

11

persons whose lying deceptiveness and impractical sentimentality has now been recognized. This new wisdom of the state, the product of the objective concept of truth supplied by naturalistic positivism, a philosophy adapted to scientifically demonstrable knowledge, may indeed be cold and unfeeling, but it is at least honest. *It* is the truth of man, set free from all idealism and its illusions.

But just as the idealistic understanding of truth fails to convince us today, so does this " truth " of positivistic realism fail to satisfy us, in spite of its scientific demonstrability. Neither does the picture of man, as it appears to us in the light of the idea, of the thinking subject, nor the picture that thrusts itself upon us as objective knowledge, grasp the truth about man. Man is not merely the knowing subject, nor merely the known object. This post-Cartesian apprehension of truth, which operates with the antithetical dichotomy of object and subject, entirely misses the essential thing, the unity of man. In the one case as in the other, it arises from a will to dominate, an attitude, so to speak, of violence, which man has learned in his intercourse with nature, and through which, obviously with great success, he attempts to seize her mysteries from her, and succeeds in doing so. But neither this dominating self, nor the nature dominated by it, is that which leads us to the truth about man.

Without any recourse to philosophy and science, everyone knows something of what we might call the manifestations of man in community: the ability to speak with one another, to understand one another, sympathy, freedom, responsibility. Sympathy, for example, participation in the life of another, in his success, in his joyful or painful experience, arises from an identification with him through feeling. As the passion of love, this identification is on the one side intensified to the highest degree, and on the other side limited in the most exclusive sense to " this one." But in both its forms, as sympathy and as the passion of love, it is accidental and biased; some people are congenial to us, others not — they leave us cold. The feelings of sympathy and love are not at the disposal of our will; we are at their mercy. Precisely the reverse is true of responsibility. We must be just to everyone and respect everyone as a person " like ourselves." Yet this universal responsibility is indeed there as a challenge, as the " Thou shalt," but not as a reality. It hovers over reality as the " moral law," but it is unconnected with being.

But now what is the truth about man? His actual being or that which he ought to be? How can we understand the riddle of which we are aware, the painful rift in our being which drove Pascal to that famous cry: " *Quelle chimère est-ce donc que l'homme? Quelle nouveauté, quel monstre, quel chaos, quel sujet de contradiction, quel prodige! Juge de toutes choses, imbécile ver de terre; dépositaire du vrai, cloaque d'incertitude et d'erreur; gloire et rebut de l'univers.*" [4] There is one form of idealism which might well be considered the most qualified to claim that it had solved the problem of the truth about man — the critical idealism of Kant. But it is precisely here that the rift is most obvious. In the *Critique of Pure Reason*, Kant had, as he thought, demonstrated that in theoretical knowledge, in the world that is given through sense and understanding, there is no place for the free and responsible man, that is, for the human man. But this first of his *Critiques*, according to his own view, had precisely the significance of leaving room for the *Critique of Practical Reason* for man as a person, as a responsible free being. Freedom is known by man in the word " Thou shalt." This imperative, however, is unconnected with being. It stands as a categorical imperative above being. Freedom and responsibility are experienced by man only in this fashion, that they are enjoined upon him. The " conception of the categorical imperative as a divine command " — which, according to Kant, is the step out of morals into religion — is not capable of bridging the gulf between the world of being and that of the imperative, and all the less so because man is severed from the divine will by the " radical evil," which is disclosed by Kant's inexorably honest analysis of the human reality. [5]

[4] Pascal, *Pensées*, Fragment 434.
[5] *Die Religion innerhalb der Grenzen der blossen Vernunft (Re-*

13

In his *opus postumum*, Kant struggles with the question whether a divine will may be postulated which confronts the human self as a reality. He never came to a clear answer to this question because his concept of autonomy held him captive within the frontiers of immanence. He was not able to take the step to faith because what was known to him, and to his time in general, as faith, was nothing but heteronomy, belief in dogma. So he came to a halt, as it were, a watcher by the threshold. It was reserved for later minds to win an understanding of faith which was unmistakably free from the odium of heteronomy, and which revealed the "Thou shalt" of the categorical imperative as reality, as the foundation of our being.

Although the post-Kantian idealistic systems were not able to hold in check the positivistic spirit of the nineteenth century, idealism was not simply "finished." Right up to the present day it has repeatedly found notable advocates, in whom at least the *question* concerning the truth about man retained its vitality, and who were able repeatedly to disclose the weaknesses of "naïve realism." Particularly from two sides it has received new impulses. First, from the side of historical scholarship. The historian could not fail to see that history is something different from the evolutionary course of natural events.[6] In his work *The Limitations of the Formation of Concepts in the Natural Sciences*, Heinrich Rickert showed that in historical happenings, in contrast to those which are the object of the natural sciences, the unique individual and not universal law is the thing of decisive importance. On the other hand, Wilhelm Dilthey made it clear that in relation to the historical object it is not so much the causal explanation as an "understanding" through a kind of identification with the object that is the indispensable presupposition of the apprehension of historical happenings. These

---

ligion *Within the Bounds of Reason Alone*), IV, "Concerning the Origin of Evil in Human Nature."

[6] J. C. Burckhardt, *Weltgeschichtliche Betrachtungen* (*Reflections on World History*), p. 23: "But history is different from nature; its productivity and creative and destructive powers are different."

14

two really irrefutable arguments, together with Edmund Husserl's "logical investigations" and the "noetic" in them, which was contrasted with all psychology, were not indeed able to subdue the domineering positive naturalistic spirit of the age but were able effectively to reduce its claims to be the only valid system.

It was just as significant that precisely from the side of the most exact and objective of all the sciences — that of physics — objectivism was called in question. In the physics of the last half century a revolutionary transformation has taken place, which has made impossible the naïvely realistic equation of objective truth with that which can be seen and touched. The visible, resting, massive surface of my writing desk became a collocation of electrons, protons, and neutrons, an electrical field, in which unceasingly processes are occurring that even the greatest physicist is unable to compute. Energies have replaced masses, mathematical formulas have replaced visible things. The drink of water that refreshes us has become the H_2O of the chemist, which the physicist further divides into an infinitely complicated system of indescribable particles of energy. When we arrive at this point it is impossible to say "what water really is." The "object" is not only infinitely strange to us, but it has become nonobjectual, a thought-thing, a *nooumenon*. Idealism — in the form that Leibniz gave to it — has again become a discussable philosophy. Further, through the concept of the system of reference that is the basis of Einstein's Theory of Relativity, the standpoint of the knowing subject, and with it the subject itself, has entered into the description of the world of objects. A new Copernican revolution has come in sight, whose results are as yet unpredictable. One thing, however, is certain: the world picture of naturalistic positivism, the infinity of space, the infinity of time, the unconditional validity of the causal principle, are no longer accepted without question but are in process of dissolution.[7]

[7] Cf. Karl Heim, *Die Wandlung im naturwissenschaftlichen Weltbild* (1951); (E. T., *The Transformation of the Scientific World View*).

But all this has only a very indirect relevance to the question concerning the truth about man. It is a different matter with the philosophy that stems directly from the intention of transcending the subject-object antithesis, and so apprehending man as a whole, the "philosophy of existence." Its main thesis is that man is neither merely the (knowing) subject, nor merely the (known) object. This is the common element in every kind of existentialism. Its first form is the philosophy of Martin Heidegger. This is a synthesis of Husserl's phenomenology, Dilthey's philosophy of history, and Kierkegaard's Christian philosophy of existence, to which it, like all the others, owes the concept of existence, of being in time. But this, in contrast to Kierkegaard, Heidegger understands as " being unto death." In the " resolve " with which man acknowledges this as the fundamental character of his existence, he achieves " authenticity " in contrast to the mass existence of " one," which consists in the evasion of this authentic existence. In his later writings Heidegger approaches nearer and nearer to an ontologism that he derives from his interpretation — to my mind a correct one — of ancient Greek *alētheia* concept, and which discontinues the theme of his earlier important work, *Being and Time* (1927) the promised second volume of which has thus never appeared.

The second form of existentialism is the philosophy of Karl Jaspers, which grew out of his "psychology of world outlooks," and seeks a synthesis of existentialism and Neo-Kantianism or Platonism. The third, which is indeed the best known and most influential, is the philosophy of Jean-Paul Sartre, who, especially through his combination of highly abstract reflection (*Being and Nothingness*), literary criticism (*Situations*), novels and dramas, has had a really sensational influence on the intellectual life of France, and, indeed, of the whole world. Although Sartre claims that his " existentialism is a humanism," what really remains as a residue of humanity in his work is only a nihilistic dissolution of everything human, and the empty assertion of absolute freedom, which is the dynamic of his destructive efforts. And to the question, What is the truth about man? he suggests with cynical irony that there is no answer.

16

All these forms are indeed descendants of Kierkegaard's existentialism. He was the original creator of the concept of existence, transcending thereby the object-subject antithesis, and apprehending man as a totality. But while Kierkegaard was able to do this only by philosophizing as a Christian because he recognized this totality not *in* man but *beyond* man, Heidegger, Jaspers, and Sartre in different ways and in varying degrees have repudiated this Christian ancestor of theirs, and so have surrendered the perspective from which this total view of man was achieved and was possible. Sartre did this by starting with atheism as an axiom; Heidegger by evading the question of God; [8] Jaspers by indeed acknowledging God in the Neoplatonic fashion as transcendent ground, but affirming him as absolute and therefore unknowable Being in contradiction to the belief in revelation,[9] whose affirmations he declares to be arrogant and, as the idealist Medicus had already declared, mythological.[10] Thus the truth about man is not to be found in the existential philosophy, either. It cannot be found at all, when we make man our point of departure.

[8] Cf. Martin Buber's postscript to his *Schriften über das dialogische Prinzip* (1954).

[9] Cf. my essay *Christlicher Glaube und Philosophie der Existenz* in the *Festschrift* for Heinrich Barth (1960), p. 119–130.

[10] Fritz Medicus, *Vom Wahren, Guten und Schönen* (1943) and *Das Mythologische in der Religion* (1944).

II

Truth
as Encounter

T HAT WE ourselves cannot find the truth about man, because
it *is* not in us and we *are* not in it — that is the point of
departure of Kierkegaard's *Philosophical Fragments*. This book,
eccentric in its form, is, together with the two volumes of the
Unscientific Postscript, the chief philosophical work of the great
Dane. It purports to be an experiment in thought, which has
set itself the task of asking what truth must be if we oppose the
Socratic idea that truth is immanent, even if only latent, in man.

Kierkegaard opposes to the basic thought of Socrates the contrary thought that the truth is not *in* man, but must come *to*
him. In the further course of the argument it appears that by
this he means the thought, expounded by him in the form of a
fairy tale or myth, that the divine truth itself has come to
humanity in the form of a man, from outside of man, and from
outside of the world, in a unique event in time, "in the
moment," "*im Augenblick.*" This event is the incarnation of
the divine Word in Jesus Christ, which can only be perceived
in the act of faith. To the elucidation of this principal thesis in
discussion with the idealism of his time (Hegel), the whole of
Kierkegaard's further lifework was dedicated. Indeed, looking
backward, Kierkegaard sees that his whole " activity as a writer "
from the beginning has served this purpose.[11]

This means that the decisive character of the historical

---

[11] The title of this book, which contains two essays, is: *The
Point of View for My Authorship* and *Concerning My Influence
as an Author.*

Current Check-Outs summary for Wise Ph.D
        Thu May 02 08:21:02 EDT 2019

BARCODE: 39353000839389
TITLE: Truth as encounter.
DUE DATE: Jun 30 2019

element in the rediscovered Christian understanding of truth had become clear. But an explanation was still lacking of the equally important second, personal element.

The being of man as person depends not on his thought but on his responsibility, upon the fact that a supreme Self calls to him and communicates Himself to him. It depends on what is called in the following chapters " responsive actuality," the claim of the Self who is Lord that is at the same time the assurance of the graciously creating and justifying Self, as it is perceived in faith. Only in this double relation, not in his rationality, has man as person his origin and fundamental being. His deepest nature consists in this " answerability," i.e., in this existence in the Word of the Creator. In this call to the Creator himself, the loving Creator who as a Thou calls us to himself, in this dependence, man is transformed from a creature of nature into a responsible, spiritually free creature, and at the same time knows that his self-sufficiency is captivity within himself, and that his actual being — not only God-given but also estranged from God — is sinful. In the call of the Creator who assures him, in his own despite, that he belongs to Him, in this Word of forgiveness and reconciliation, his original being is given to him anew. In the call of the sovereign Self he perceives this double dependence, this being whose origin and goal is God.[12]

This perception is what the Bible calls faith, and in this perceiving faith, in this responsive actuality, consists his specific, his personally responsible being. The being of man as a person is thus at bottom not a being like that of an object present to the senses — as objectivism claims — nor yet — as subjectivism says — an original, underivative, unconditional freedom. There is, indeed, a certain analogy between Kant's conception that personal being can only be grasped as freedom under the imperative and what we said about responsibility. For the imperative is indeed the expression of responsibility. And yet this impera-

[12] Cf. my *Dogmatics*, Vol. III, especially chs. 11, " Faith and Unbelief," and 14, " The Perfected Form of Faith: The Justification of the Sinner by Faith Alone."

tive is in Kant immanent in the rational self. It does not stem from a claim and an assurance coming from beyond the man's self. Responsibility is for him not a relationship but something immanent; responsibility not only *for* oneself — which it is in faith also — but responsibility *to* oneself, which annuls the very concept of *responsibility*. The contradiction between the doctrine of radical evil and that of autonomy is obvious. Therefore, from the standpoint of faith, which is understood as a relation to a claim and an assurance, the concept of autonomy is nothing else than this self-enclosure which produces the solitude of the self, and perverts our nature, making it unnatural. The assertion of un-conditional freedom is, from the Christian point of view, the root of all evil, original sin. Either man is in the last resort dependent, or he is in the last resort independent; either he *has* a master, or he is his own master.

But where will this divine Thou that is the foundation of our being become a real Thou who speaks to us in claim and in assurance? Where does this truth of man become event? To this question the answer of faith says: In history and, in fact, in that history where the supreme Self that makes us responsible, himself so confronts us that he at the same time claims us and gives himself to us. This point in history is Jesus, who is known in faith as the Christ, the *kyrios*. There one stands before us who is indeed a real, human Thou, but in whose being and action the gap between what is and what ought to be is not present, in whose person those different " characteristics of humanity " of which we spoke above can be understood as a unity, the man dependent upon God as the man obedient to God. This is he who as the One responsible knows himself to be identical with the Will that makes him responsible, and therefore the One in whose self the divine Self speaks to us, whose claims are a divine commandment, whose forgiving love is God's forgiveness. Here is not merely sympathy, but the love that bestows itself in obedience, suffering for sinful humanity. Here is not the self-assertive will to power, but the obedient will to self-sacrifice.

Therefore, the knowledge of this act as God's act is at the

20

same time man's self-knowledge as a sinner, and the knowledge of the new personal being as sonship of God. To know him in trustful obedience is not only to *know* the truth, but through God's self-communication to *be* in it, in the truth that as love is at the same time fellowship. The truth about man is founded in the divine humanity of Christ, which we apprehend in faith in Christ, the Word of God. This is truth as encounter. So to encounter him as he challenges and permits us to do, means to encounter the Sovereign, the Self who is Lord, and to know his self-sacrifice on the cross as the act of God, and to be translated into the love that calls us in our own despite to itself, and names us sons and heirs of his eternal life. In this believing knowledge and trustful and obedient acceptance of this Word and Act, our original personality, which is based upon God's creative and self-giving love, is restored and known anew as our authentic truth, and that false freedom of autonomy, that self which has its truth in itself, is known as a lie. Here *truth happens*, here we *are* in the truth, which is not in us but comes to us, which makes us free by restoring to us our true being, our being in the Thou, and our being for the Thou. In this truth as encounter, in which we understand our personal being as being in the love of the Creator and Redeemer — and not only understand it but have it as a new bestowal of our original being — to have and to be are one.[13] Therefore, to understand this Word of God that has become a person is at the same time to understand oneself as a person. And to understand oneself thus (in Him) is at the same time to understand one another as brothers, as children of the one Father, who in this Word and Deed of his communicates himself as the Creator. We proceed to deal with the different elements in rather more detail.

1. The first and decisive element is the historical, the truth that is not in us but comes to us. This is what is most offensive to the autonomous reason. But the offense continues only so long as we are held captive in the " Thou-less " thinking of the solitary self. The exclusion from the Thou that is the foundation of our being makes us solitary, gives our thinking the character

[13] Cf. Gabriel Marcel, *Etre et Avoir* (1935).

21

of a monologue. But reason, as the word "comprehension" indicates, could be something different, namely, com-prehension, taking into our grasp.[14] But since in fact we are so locked off from the Thou, this lock, as it were, must be forced open. And it is precisely this that happens in the encounter with him in whom the Word which has established our being comes to meet us anew. That this truth must be a historical truth, i.e., that it encounters us as a truth that comes from outside of us, is due to the fact that we ourselves are not able, in our own power and in our own initiative, to find our way back to this Thou-Word on which our existence is founded and to break open this locked self.

But it does not seem so much to be the historical element as such that causes offense as the "localized character," the exclusive uniqueness and singularity of this historical element. Why only here, why not also there, why not in all history? This is the objection of German historico-philosophical idealism, especially of Hegel. Our answer is: This is so, because only the event, the localized historical event, is this thing "outside of ourselves," and because conversely all this generalization, this anti-intolerance, is nothing but a cloak for the circumvention of the historical as event. "History in general" is nothing more than just man himself once more, man the self-sufficient, man who needs nothing outside himself, the autarky and autonomy of the nonreceptive reason.[15]

2. Truth as encounter is the Word of the Thou which opens the self-enclosed self. It is not the thought-logos of the Greeks, but the communicative word through which the self is once more restored to the position that befits it, through which it

14 TRANSLATOR'S NOTE: Here there is in the German a really untranslatable wordplay, which can only be partially presented by the word "comprehension." *Ver-nunft* comes from the two roots, *Ver*, here meaning "completely," and *nehmen*, "to take or receive." Brunner's intention is to show that "reason," which seems to point to autonomy, in its original meaning signifies "receiving completely," or "into our grasp" — from Another.

15 TRANSLATOR'S NOTE: The wordplay again. German, "*nicht-vernehmende Vernunft.*"

22

again becomes a com-prehending self dependent on the Thou, and resting upon its foundation. It is the self-communication of the true Thou without which we cannot be true selves. "The First Person," as we say in grammar, is the I that alone can truly say, "I," because he alone is independent, self-sufficient, without other foundation, and self-positing. This I discloses itself as an I by addressing us as Thou. And we, "the Second Person" through the word "Thou" of his address spoken to us, become true selves dependent on the Self.

The Greeks were right when they called the logos the principle of truth. But insofar as they philosophized, they understood this logos as reason or meaning, as thought and not as communication. But true humanity is not thought, or the expression of thoughts, but impartation, communication. However, this does not happen in our life. What is here communicated has the character of the communication of *something*, and this is a word that has only accidentally the form of communication. True communication would be self-communication. But it is precisely this which we are unable and unwilling to undertake. We are hindered from giving to the other, the Thou, a part of ourselves by our incurable imprisonment in ourselves. When we merely communicate "something" to another, we merely say to him what he could know of himself; we merely give up to our neighbor what we have, and not what we are. Communication in the strict sense, however, would be communication of that which is the mystery of the self. But this we cannot communicate, because we ourselves do not know it or do not wish to surrender ourselves. True self-communication would be self-dedication, the word that is one with the act of self-giving. This has happened only once in history, in the history of Him who was able to say, "For even the Son of man came not to be ministered unto, but to minister, and to give his life a ransom for many" (Mark 10:45).

But the word "Thou" in which that Self communicates himself to us is truly something that we cannot say to ourselves. It is the Word of God, the claim and assurance of the Transcendent, which, precisely because it is that truth which

23

discloses itself only in claim and assurance, is not a Transcendent Entity, nor Transcendence, as the self-enclosed reason names it, but the Person who addresses us himself, and of whom consequently we cannot speak in the neuter, but only in the form I–Thou: I thy Lord, thou my creature; Thou my Father, I thy child.

This is not *anthropo*morphism, which would violate the infinity, the unconditional and absolute character of transcendence, by forcing the ineffable into the human form of speech, and so robbing it of its absoluteness. Rather, is it the *theo*morphism of the divine self-revelation in the man Jesus Christ, who reveals the basis of our responsibility and our sonship of God in spite of ourselves. It is precisely the rigor of God's truth that is given expression by the avoidance of all impersonal terms and the acknowledgment of the figure of human personality and of communication between men as the only adequate form of speech.[16]

Truth as encounter is not truth about something, not even truth about something mental, about ideas. Rather is it that truth which breaks in pieces the impersonal concept of truth and mind, truth that can be adequately expressed *only* in the I–Thou form. All use of impersonal terms to describe it, the divine, the transcendent, the absolute, is indeed the inadequate way invented by the thinking of the solitary self to speak of it — or, more correctly, of Him.

3. Thus the historical and personal character of this truth as encounter are necessarily connected together. It is no accident that in the Bible, the witness to this truth, God is always spoken of in the I–Thou or Thou–I form. In this a double antithesis to abstraction is manifest, the antithesis to the ahistorical abstractness of the idea, which has neither beginning

[16] Cf. Karl Barth, *Kirchliche Dogmatik*, I, 1, 139: "The form in which reason communicates with reason, person with person, is language, so too when it is God's language . . . primarily in analogy with what happens in the corporeal or natural sphere. . . . The Word of God . . . is a rational and not an irrational event." (E.T., I, 1, 152.)

24

nor end, and the antithesis to impersonal knowledge of things, to the truths of thought that require no communication to a Thou, but are the product of the solitary self.

a. The thinking of reason in the traditional sense is ahistorical. It deals with substantives and not with verbs. In philosophy the substantive dominates, but in the Bible the verb, the word expressing activity. The word of God is always word and deed, history. Conversely, in philosophy, history is an alien and an embarrassment. Neither the Hindu philosophy of the Vedanta nor that of the Greeks knows the theme of history. Only through Christianity did it enter into philosophy,[17] but even here this happened only in appearance. The philosophy of history, of German idealism (Hegel), does not take this theme really seriously, for it only unfolds what is already implicit in logic. The historical element in the Neo-Hegelianism of a Croce has only the negative significance of the transience, the relativity, of all truth. The same is true of the existentialism of Heidegger; history is "being unto death," while, according to Heidegger, the truth is the timeless being of ontology.

b. This brings us to the second antithesis to Christian truth, the abstractness of the impersonal. Like history, personalism is an alien and an embarrassment in philosophy, for one cannot think a person.[18] The thinking of the solitary self regards the person, like the individual, as something that impairs truth as idea, holding to the proposition *omnis determinatio est negatio.*[19] It must consequently regard the Christian personal concept as anthropomorphism. The Bible, on the other hand, regards precisely man's personal quality as his existence in the image of *God.* God is he who reveals himself in word and deed, the unconditionally personal One. "I, and none other, am Jahweh." "*I* am the way, the truth, and the life." This Self is the truth of which the Bible, alone among the sacred scriptures

[17] Cf. Wilhelm Windelband, *Handbook of the History of Philosophy,* par. 21, "The Problem of World History."
[18] Cf. my "Personality and Person" in the *Festschrift* in honor of Emeritus Rector Dr. Hans Fischer, Verlag Schüle AG (1952).
[19] Spinoza, *Epistol.* 59.

of the peoples, speaks. This Self is its theme, "the name of God." The decisive thing in the Bible is not the monotheism, but the personalism of its concept of God. This reaches its culmination in the fact that the revelation which transcends every prophetic word is the *Incarnation* of the Word. The core of the gospel is not a Christ idea, but the message, the Word concerning him, the *Kyrios Christos*, concerning his life, passion, and death, which proves itself God's word and deed in the resurrection. This is the absolute antithesis of all abstraction. To speak in the abstract of Christ is not to speak of Jesus, the real Christ. The touchstone of faith and unbelief is the issue whether one is ashamed of this name, or speaks of it as the truth.

The person is that which cannot be universalized, nor grasped in abstractions, and it alone is the radically nonabstract entity. That the Logos of whom the Bible speaks is not speech about something, but the Speaker himself — this is the offensive thing to the solitary rational self that is cut off from the Word of the Thou. For this self the proposition holds: the more general, the more spiritual. This abstract spirit triumphs in mathematics, the most abstract of the sciences.

In diametrical antithesis to this abstract concept of truth stands the truth that is identical with self-communication, with love. It is therefore the boldest word of personalism, that God is love. *This* is the truth with which the Bible deals. And this is just as much the truth about God as the truth about man. Because and insofar as he has lost this truth, man is inhuman, and all inhumanity has in this its origin. This inhumanity is the same thing as the absence of the Thou or the solitude of the self.

4. Thus the Word, personal being, and love belong together. Love, not justice! Whereas love speaks to the heart, and is directed to the person in its concreteness, justice has a neutral, impersonal, rational character. The Greeks knew all about the justice that obtains in the world, and this is indeed the objective principle of all ordered society. But they knew nothing of *agapē*, of self-surrendering, self-bestowing, uncaused love. When Paul speaks of the "righteousness of God," he always means thereby the love of God that is freely bestowed in Christ ("without the

26

works of the law "), and the believer's justification or sonship of God accomplished by Him alone. In contrast with the principle "justice" — which everyone understands as the correspondence of work done and reward, as rational equity of treatment without regard for persons — love, which is bestowed on us in Christ, is just as undeserved as it is irrational, and precisely not intelligible, precisely not in accordance with general rules, but spontaneous and individual in its application.[20] Here only the pronoun of the first and second person, not an "it" but only I–Thou is the possible adequate form of expression. "*I* have chosen *thee, thou* art mine." Therefore in faith in Christ a new self is born, the self that we do not find in ourselves, but which is only bestowed on us in faith in him.

Only in the knowledge of him who can speak to us with authority because he himself is what he demands, and who in the suffering of death upon the cross bestows upon us what he demands, namely self-bestowing love, only in this knowledge is this I–Thou word audible as the voice of the Father, which in our own hearts describes him as our true self. The justification of the sinner is the perfect form of faith, in which the I–Thou of the divine human truth becomes reality, the truth of the Christ, which is identical with the truth of faith.[21] Only in this event is the divine Self revealed as the origin of our human self. Indeed, more than this: in this event our human self is constituted, and when this happens, "the new man" knows that this is his original being. He knows himself as created in and for the Word of God, that God who, as the divine Self, is our real Thou.

5. In the light of this fundamental communication, however, communication itself, self-communicating love, is disclosed as the meaning of human life, and existence in love is disclosed as the decisive life-act. The reception of the divine love necessitates an activity of love; from the religious root grows the moral act as its natural necessary consequence. It is

[20] Cf. my *Dogmatics* III, ch. 22, "The Commandment of Love and the Law."
[21] Cf. my *Dogmatics* III, ch. 14.

27

not the following of a legal prescription that is the truly moral thing, i.e., our right behavior in intercourse with our fellowmen, but *living* among them, with them, for them, the active radiation, the love that streams forth from God, a life *lived* with one another, in that element which we have received as our true being. And, conversely, now every human encounter becomes an encounter with God, even in the sense that the encounter with our fellowman, whatever his intention in it may be, becomes a divine gift to us, a proof of God's love and a claim that comes from God the Lord.

6. There remains still one last important element of truth as encounter, to which attention must be drawn. This truth cannot be *held*, or possessed. Its nature is, rather, such that it takes possession of us, " lays hold of us." Here is to be seen at its clearest the antithesis to the knowing that is represented as an act of taking possession. The truth with which faith is concerned can only be received. It is therefore identical with grace. (John 1:17.) Early truth can be had, possessed. But the truth of faith is not of this piecemeal, fragmentary character. Being is of the essence of faith. " To be in the truth," " to be in the Word," " to dwell in love," " to be in Christ " — this is the only New Testament way of speaking. And this expresses its existential character. " To be in . . ." is a phrase that relates to the totality of man, in contrast to the phrase " to have." This was, indeed, the point of departure of Kierkegaard's *Fragments* — that we do not have the truth because we *are* not in the truth, and this is precisely what the New Testament says about man. It is true that the Word of God is the creative origin of our being. But we have fallen away from it and are excluded from it by our own act of self-closure, by the fact that we seek the truth in ourselves, in the solitude of the self, and in the estrangement of our " autonomous reason " from the Thou. *Hence* the lovelessness of mere reason, *hence* the antithesis between reason and heart, *hence* the contradiction between the good as obligation, and the good as love flowing from the heart.[22]

[22] This antithesis, which at the same time affirms as Idea what is denied, finds clear expression in Kant, *Critique of Practical Reason*

In faith in Christ, i.e., in the love of God that communicates itself to us, this antagonism is overcome. For the good is identical with the true in the receiving of the divine love, which makes us human, in the grace, which is the same thing as the truth ("grace and truth came by Jesus Christ," John 1:17), which makes us members of one body (I Cor., ch. 12), which makes us that ecclesia whose vital source and goal is the Christ, who gave himself up for us, who "took upon him what was ours, that he might give us what is his" (Irenaeus).

We remember what we said (p. 12) about manifestations of man in community. In these there is an obscure knowledge about what is truly human, which nowhere appears in our experience as a totality and as a unity, but only as the *disjecta membra* of such a totality. But here in Jesus Christ, as he is known in faith, is given the "missing center," which makes these manifestations a whole. Here the truth shows itself, the Logos of God as grace, as love bestowed, which makes all who are apprehended by it into "one body," where every member suffers along with every other one ("sympathy") and where the gift of every member becomes a task to perform for the whole, for the body. In this body every one knows himself a member that needs the other, and understands the gift given to him as a task, as responsibility for the other and for the whole, the body. But the Spirit that creates this body, like the responsibility, has his origin in the divine Thou; he is the self-communicating Thou. He is therefore the Spirit of freedom (II Cor. 3:17), who makes us free from the law by bringing each of us under the immediate sovereignty of God, binding him directly and exclusively to himself, the Lord, so that we become "mirrors" in which the nature of God is visible in reflected form — and always imperfectly — as *agapē*. Here responsibility

---

(Cassirer, pp. 91–93): "Love to God is impossible. . . . For a command to like to do a thing is itself contradictory . . . and no creature can ever reach this stage of moral disposition. . . . Love, which apprehends no inner reluctance of the will toward the law . . . would cease to be virtue. Such a love would be 'religious enthusiasm'" (Kant's *Theory of Ethics*, Abbott, pp. 176–177).

29

(as dependent on God), is identical with freedom (as belonging to God), just as sympathy, the power to suffer with others, is identical with the joyful and triumphant participation in the *gloria Dei,* in victory over the world and the " care of the world."

III

Truth
as Encounter and Science[23]

HOW THEN does it stand with science and its truth if truth
as encounter stands above it — that truth in which responsibility has its foundation? This truth is neither scientific
nor metaphysical. Both metaphysics as known to Aristotle and
speculation as known to Platonic and post-Kantian idealism are
products of the thinking of the solitary self. It is, rather, that
truth which comes from the Thou, which is the origin of our
personal being as " responsive actuality," [24] as true re-*sponsibility*. Responsibility conscientiousness is a charge also upon the

[23] By the term " science " here only natural science is meant,
i.e., all sciences insofar as they acknowledge the criteria of natural
science as their own also. The profound difference between natural
science and the mental sciences (*Geisteswissenschaften*) has been
expounded by Rickert and Dilthey. For the problem " Faith and
Science " in the special form it takes in relation to the mental
sciences, I must refer to my *Revelation and Reason*, which was not
written until some years after the present book, and was published
in 1943. In it some of the questions that at present dominate
theological discussion are anticipated and treated throughout on
the basis of the insights gained by *The Divine-Human Encounter*.
Here I intentionally refrained from making reference to the philosophy of Heidegger. (Cf. my essay " Theologie und Ontologie," in
Zeitschrift für Theologie und Kirche, Neue Folge 12, No. 2.) Since
that time (1931) the problems have been dealt with in much
greater detail by other authors.

[24] Cf. my anthropology, *Der Mensch im Widerspruch*, p. 88
(E.T., *Man in Revolt*, pp. 97–98), where this concept is expounded
for the first time. From then onward it occurs repeatedly in my
writings as a technical term, " responsive actuality."

natural scientist, which lies upon his actions, as upon all human actions, and alone constitutes their human and interpersonal character.

Does this extra- or supra-scientific perspective do full justice to science, without curtailment or falsification? The two truths, the "ethical" and the "scientific," are different, inasmuch as the one has to do with the sphere of the historical and personal, with that of the I–Thou relationship, and the other with that of the impersonal, the I–It relationship. The attempt to understand the personal world as a function of the world of things breaks down for the reason that here, in the world of things, we cannot find that which makes persons persons, and determines the relation between persons as such. So that the reverse relation, the primacy of the personal, can be the only possible one. Under these extra- and supra-scientific presuppositions how is science conceivable? Has it the necessary freedom for development within the limits set to it by responsibility?

So long as Christian truth is understood in the sense given to it by the orthodox understanding of faith, conflict is inevitable, or the dualism of a "double truth" remains the one unsatisfactory "solution." By reason of its encroachments into the domain of knowledge, the truth of faith meets with the justified resistance of science, as the classical examples of Galileo and Darwin show. But the converse is also possible, and happens in the formation of modern pseudoscientific myths, such as that of pan-causalism and that of infinite space and infinite time. But if Christian truth is understood in the sense of truth as encounter, then there is no attempt to keep science in leading strings or to compete with it, nor is there a degeneration of science into a "scientific world outlook." The self-critical scientist does not claim that all reality is apprehended by his categories, especially by those of substance and causality. His supreme principle is that of "openness to reality," by which the possibility is envisaged that there may conceivably be reality of an extracausal, extrasubstantial kind, on which it is beyond his competence to deliver judgment.

32

The scientist of today can no longer come before the world as an Ernst Haeckel or the elder Huxley did, in the confidence of one who through his science has in principle solved "the riddles of the universe." To him, precisely through the advance of science in the nineteenth and twentieth centuries, these riddles have become much more enigmatic, so that he is rather in danger of becoming a skeptic who entirely despairs of their solution. He has once more an inkling that as a scientist he will never be able to master precisely those problems which concern man as man. He looks round for some extrascientific reality that might be able to throw some light for him on his own life problem. He recognizes that science is not in a position to solve his life problem, which is ethical, since science can neither give an account of responsibility nor of the problem of human community, nor of the problem of the meaning of his own action. But these questions pose themselves with irresistible urgency, so to speak, on the threshold between his laboratory and his house. There are therefore today not a few who as scientists are open to faith, provided only that this faith does not through a dogma violently invade their scientific territory. Today there are again leading men of science such as Max Planck, W. K. Heisenberg, and Arthur Compton who confess the Christian faith, and in so doing, leave in principle to others the reflection about the reality that encounters them in faith, knowing the frontiers that are set for them as scientists; their science makes them modest. They acknowledge the legitimacy, perhaps even the necessity, of theology as a service that is performed representatively for other fellowmen, inasmuch as in it theologians reflect about the basis and meaning of responsibility and human community, which they also regard as a standing obligation upon them. But they keep a vigilant watch lest this reflection overstep its own boundaries, as does orthodox theology, and enunciate pseudoscientific theses as dogmas of faith, as it has done often enough in the past.

Thus a self-critical science, and a self-critical theology that understands itself as reflection about the ground of responsibility, do not stand in a mutually contradictory, but in a complementary, relation. But that theology is self-critical whose only formal principle is that of openness to reality, which brings with it no material presuppositions of any kind, whose understanding of truth is consequently that of truth as encounter. But the point where the questioner as mere questioner and the questioner as one called in question meet each other is the doctrine of man, anthropology.

For natural science, man on the one hand, in the vertical classification of the Linnaean system as the species Homo sapiens, is one of the primates, the highest animal type; on the other hand, in the temporal horizontal evolutionary series, the latest member in the evolution of species, more precisely, the latest evolved of the mammals. This evolutionary line, considered from without, is above all characterized by the relative size and differentiation of the brain; considered from within, by the increase of consciousness. Man as man came into existence with the moment — which cannot exactly be specified — in which the decisive step was taken from consciousness in general to self-consciousness.

For faith, or for the man reflecting about faith, this self-consciousness, this self, is the answer to the Thou that calls forth the self, the answering re-sponsible self. Man is not understandable in himself, but only in terms of this call. This is his grandeur, that he can only be understood as that which he is in the light of God. "*L'homme passe infiniment l'homme.*" (Pascal.) [25] *This* is the essential thing, not his origin from the evolution of species. To understand what man is, we must start from his divine *principium*, and not from his temporal *initium*, not with the prehuman becoming man, but with God becoming man in Jesus Christ. This is man's true beginning, that history of which the Prologue to John's Gospel speaks, " In the beginning was the Word." In this Logos, man as a person has his origin. And this Logos is not the one of which Greek idealism or, indeed, idealism in general, speaks — the ahistorical timeless logos of speculative thinking — but the Logos that became history in Jesus Christ, the Logos in which the Word of God,

[25] *Pensées*, Fragment 434.

34

God's very self, the Lord, calls to us and encounters us. In this truth as encounter, man has his creative origin, in that Word which " calls to what is not, that it may be " (Rom. 4:17).

Here it becomes clear that man is neither a mere object, nor a subject intelligible in itself, but responsive actuality, answering, responsible person. Only from this central point are those "manifestations of man in community," which we mentioned earlier, intelligible: language as something fundamentally different from animal communication by signs, namely, as self-communication, responsibility as something fundamentally different from the protection of self-interest and the interest of the species; love, in which man becomes truly human, as something fundamentally different from the sex instinct or *erōs*. Faith in the Thou who speaks to us in love is faith in God, the Creator, whom neither naturalism nor idealism can know. This God is the Creator of everything that science knows as the reality of nature, in the sense of everything perceived by the senses. In the knowledge of the Thou over against me, the whole world of objects and causal processes is included, while it is at the same time infinitely transcended.

The man who believes he is compelled on scientific grounds to look on himself as an insignificant piece of the infinite universe must simply feel lost in this world he inhabits, in which he is a mere nothing and in which his longing for true love must remain unsatisfied. In it he is the solitary man who despairs in his solitude. But this despair and lostness disappears in the knowledge that the Word of love has created this immense world and governs it, even if the manner of this *creatio* and *gubernatio* remains a mystery to us, and, so long as we live in this world, will remain a mystery. Faith in the Christ, who encounters us in revelation's word about the Christ, illuminates the darkness of this mystery, making it " the true light that lighteth every man " (John 1:9). In him faith recognizes the "Word that was in the beginning," the origin of all things and at the same time " the firstborn of many brethren " (Rom. 8:29), who makes us responsible, who makes us dependent, and at the same time gives us a Master to whom we belong, whose true being is self-bestowing love, and who discloses in it the meaning of our being.[26]

These two worlds, the causal and the personal, meet together in the person of man, become one in his action. It is our daily, hourly experience that human persons use the causal and mechanical system as means. The heartfelt letter of consolation that I write to a fellow human being in trouble is typed on the typewriter according to the rigid causal laws. This "miracle" that mind and heart use causal and material means is scientifically incomprehensible. *That* it happens in our continual experience, *how* it happens, how the loving will and thought of a person brings about the movement of particles in space, remains a mystery to us, into which the scientist can penetrate only a little way, but which he will never fathom, because the unity of the person will never be the object of science. Here the word *"ignoramus ignorabimus"* uttered by one of the greatest physiologists, Dubois-Reymond, still holds good after all the advances of physiology in the last hundred years. The scientist must indeed defend the causal principle against all romantic organic concepts as the working hypothesis valid for him, but can never dogmatically declare it to be the knowledge that explains everything.

But we continually experience also the contrary of this, that the causal world senselessly and unfeelingly breaks into the personal world, and, finally, in the event of death, brings personal life to an end — as far as our knowledge goes. As to what happens beyond the frontier of our knowledge, science can offer no valid comment, but faith can. Its utterances have indeed in no sense a scientific, objective significance or certainty, but they do have the certainty of truth as encounter in their own context. "For I am persuaded that neither death, nor life, nor angels, nor principalities . . . nor powers, nor height, nor depth, nor any other creature, shall be able to separate us from the love of God, which is in Christ Jesus our Lord." (Rom. 8:38 ff.) At the same place where the decisive knowledge about our personal being is to be found and is found — a knowledge

26 Cf. my *Dogmatics* III, ch. 11, on re-sponsibility.

36

not of a scientific objective, but of a personal, kind — the question is also answered about what lies beyond the frontier of death, through the truth that encounters us in Christ, a truth that is identical with faith in Christ. In the same way the question of conscience is not answered either through objective science or through the knowledge of the subject and the idea, but only through faith in him in whom the divine-human truth encounters us.

To understand science in the light of faith is to understand it instrumentally as a means that serves the person and the personal world. To understand it as the final truth, as truth absolutely, is to degrade persons to things, and, theologically speaking, to make science a superstition hostile to personal being. It becomes then an atheistic anti-God, the antihumanism of the pseudoscientific ideology and tyranny. It is true that the church's false concept of faith is not without blame for this whole subversion of the order of values; indeed, on the contrary, it bears a principal share of the blame. By misunderstanding faith as belief in dogma, and the Bible, in which the witness to the past Word of God reaches us, as infallible, and a "holy book," it stands in irreconcilable contradiction both to true faith in Christ and to science.

Genuine faith, however, which in the Bible itself is described by the word "pistis" — trust — is a faith that frees and releases the human spirit from all prejudices. It does not contradict the causal investigations of natural science and its evolutionism. For evolution is the way and manner in which God causes both the individual man to develop from the embryo (Ps. 139) and also the species Homo sapiens from the evolution of species. The nature that God has created and creates does not make any leaps, not even a leap from the prehuman to the human. The gradual development of the forms of life, which covers hundreds of millions of years, leads imperceptibly to the point where from the consciousness that is presumably common to all stages of living beings, but certainly to the highest, there originates the self-consciousness of man, who is aware both of himself and, at the same time, of the Thou.

37

But it is a part of the mystery of man as man, as person, that in this Word of Christ he perceives not only his divine origin but at the same time his revolt against this origin of his, his "fall." The Word of Christ discloses to us not only the *grandeur* but also the *misère de l'homme*. Man is not only the being created by God's Word but also the being estranged from his origin. And indeed this estrangement occurs precisely in the self-affirmation with which man answers, or rather does not answer, the divine call to him, choosing rather to assert himself by misunderstanding the divine call as his own word, as his autonomy. This is the profound "self-misunderstanding of reason" (Hamann), in which the whole *misère de l'homme* has its origin and the law of its nature, or rather of the perversion of its nature. This self is the autonomous self, which denies its origin in the self-communicating supreme Self of the Creator [27] and claims that its self is uncreated, without beginning, unbestowed, and autonomous, the rebellious self, which tears itself away from its true origin, the self-emancipating self. Instead of saying "Thou," it says defiantly, "I, I myself." This is the origin of the disastrous history of mankind.

Both, the *grandeur* and the *misère* of man, inextricably interwoven with each other, form the fabric of human history, which, although scarcely then noticeable, differentiates itself from the natural process of evolution on the first appearance of self-consciousness, and is inseparable from man's being. "History is the break with this nature by means of the awakening consciousness." (Jacob Burckhardt.) [28] The being of man is historical, and can only be understood as historical.

[27] Cf. J. G. Fichte, *Die Anweisung zum seligen Leben* (Auswahl in 6 Bänden, *Verlag F. Meiner*, Leipzig, pp. 191 and 192): "The hypothesis of a Creation" is "the absolute and fundamental error of all false metaphysics and religious teaching . . . , for it is quite impossible to produce a clear concept of a Creation such as is necessary for real thought, and no one has ever yet done so." "The assumption of a Creation is the first test of falsity." "In the beginning was the Word, the Logos, which could also be rendered as 'Reason.'"
[28] *Weltgeschichtliche Betrachtungen*, p. 24.

But the Word of God that encounters us in Jesus Christ does more than uncover the human mystery. It calls us back to our divine origin and in an inconceivable manner restores us to the " status " for which the divine love had intended us from the beginning. The Word of God in Christ is the word of forgiveness and restoration, in which the event of the cross can be perceived as word and deed of God, and in faith is apprehended as such, or rather, apprehends us. This *recapitulatio* (Irenaeus) of the original Word is the theme of the Bible. Only in this act and Word, only in this history, is the mystery of man revealed, while elsewhere it is indeed obscurely felt but at the same time misunderstood. Neither from the standpoint of naturalistic nor from that of idealistic evolutionism is man seen correctly, without illusion, without curtailment and falsification, but only in the light of that divine-human history. He is never a mere object, nor yet a subject intelligible in himself and by himself, but a " responsive actuality."

This Christological anthropology, which is accessible only to faith, includes (in principle) within itself the insights of naturalistic objectivism and idealistic subjectivism, but at the same time excludes (in principle) their errors. In it is given the center that shows these manifestations in their unity, but at the same time also their opposition, the inhuman demonic element. Only from this point outside himself can man know himself for what he is, as responsible person in fellowship, and for what, in antithesis to the truth, he actually is, the solitary self, the sinful man. This knowledge, however, is not theoretic but ethical, and is only to be gained by the commitment of one's own person. Faith in the Thou that speaks to us in the love of Christ is faith in the Creator of the whole world, of whom neither naturalism nor idealism can know, faith in the Creator of all that science acknowledges as the reality of nature. At the same time it is faith in the Redeemer, who " makes all things new " in the Kingdom of God.

If the knowledge that the infinite universe is there only through and for the knowing mind was described by Kant as a " Second Copernican Revolution," the much more revolutionary knowledge of faith, of truth as encounter, is that this cosmos is there through and for the Word that comes in Jesus Christ to man, who has lost it, and recovers it in faith in the Christ. Faith in this Word of Christ knows that this world is ruled by the will of God its Creator, who speaks to us in Jesus Christ as his sons, and makes us sons, as " citizens " and " heirs " of the yet invisible world of the consummation, which we now know only in faith, and of which we are only able to speak stammeringly, but which " then " we shall behold as the only true world. " But to us there is but one God, the Father, of whom are all things, and we in him, and one Lord Jesus Christ, by whom are all things, and we by him." (I Cor. 8:6.) In this word, Christian anthropology is concentrated in its essence. Truth as encounter contains the evolutionism of science within it, but leaves it infinitely far behind, as it discloses itself as a Christological theanthropology, which broadens out into the doctrine of the consummation of man in the coming Kingdom of God. Therefore the truth that encounters us is a criticism of the contemporary theology that surrenders to the skepticism of the *Zeitgeist* the hope for the future that is an essential ingredient of the New Testament witness of faith.

IV

Conclusions

1. THEOLOGY BEYOND BARTH AND BULTMANN [29]

THE MESSAGE of the Bible is the knowledge of the coming
God, of him "who is and who was and who is to come "
(Rev. 1:8). Truth as encounter is in conflict with the truth of
naturalism, the doctrine of evolution, and in conflict with
idealism, the doctrine of eternal being. It is the doctrine of the
truth that comes to man, which gives him a place in this
coming, and in it makes him new. This fundamental theme
begins to be audible in the Old Testament, but is only given its
clear and consummated form in the New Testament, in the
witness to Jesus the Christ, whose coming had been foretold.
But in the clash with the intellectual world of the Greeks, it
was most profoundly altered by orthodox theology, which did
indeed preserve the historical and eschatological element in the
teaching about Jesus the Christ, but dislodged it from the center,
replacing it by its trinitarian and two-nature doctrines.[30] The
theology of the Reformers at the beginning restored it to the
central point, but soon again itself turned into orthodoxy.

It was an event of the greatest significance when Karl Barth,
soon after the end of the First World War, when the faith of
the Reformers seemed about to be extinguished, had the courage
in his *Letter to the Romans* once more to take the Biblical
message seriously. In so doing he linked up with the Biblicism

[29] Cf. also the " Excursus: On the Contemporary Theological
Situation " in my *Dogmatics* III, pp. 248 ff. (E.T., pp. 213 ff.).

[30] Cf. my *Dogmatics* III, ch. 15, " Justifying Faith in Christ and
the Creed of the Church."

of the "Swabian Fathers," especially the two Blumhardts, Johann Christoph the father, and Christoph the son, and in accomplishing this the Christian existentialism of Søren Kierkegaard, in its opposition to the idealism of Hegel, did him invaluable service.

These were the beginnings of his theology. At that time Karl Barth, adopting a word of Kierkegaard, used to speak of theology as "the little pinch of cinnamon," and would have energetically repudiated all thought of a theological system. But soon there came a turning point in his thinking. This time, too, as in the age of Protestant orthodoxy, the thing happened quite imperceptibly through a change of emphasis in the understanding of faith. It began with the adoption of the ancient Catholic doctrine *natus ex Maria Virgine*. This myth plays an insignificant part in the New Testament witness to Christ. Neither Paul nor John nor any other of the apostolic writings proclaim the Son of God as one begotten in a supernatural manner. This substantialist understanding of the truth of God that encounters us in Jesus Christ is alien to them, and still more so the belief that in this "miracle" we apprehend the thing of decisive importance for faith in Jesus Christ. The truth of God that encounters us in Jesus the Christ has no relation to this, nor do the oldest Confessions of the Christian fellowship make any mention of the virgin birth.[31] The truth that authenticates itself in our conscience has been replaced by a supernatural *fact*, which "must be believed" on the strength of authority. This

[31] According to RGG [3] III, p. 169, "The New Testament throughout entirely takes for granted and presupposes the real, full humanity of Jesus. Only two passages, Matt., ch. 1, and Luke, ch. 1, are exceptions to this universal rule. Here we encounter the motif of generation through the Spirit, the fatherless birth. The significance of generation through the Spirit is meant to express the theological significance, the dignity of the One begotten by God. . . ." Matt., ch. 1, and Luke, ch. 1, " stand and fall with the credibility of these texts, which in the total context of the synoptic representation of history must be termed very precarious, if not impossible." On the oldest primitive forms of the Apostles' Creed, cf. RGG [2] I, columns 414 ff.

was the point from which long ago the transformation of the confession of the ancient church took its departure. It was in the direction of this "faith" that the dogma of the church developed as the doctrine of the Triune God and of the two natures in Christ. It was this doctrine, summarized in the Creed, which Karl Barth from 1924 onward expounded in his *Dogmatics* as the subject of belief. The change showed itself in three symptoms.

a. His adherence to the orthodox teachers of the seventeenth century became continually more marked. Heppe's *Dogmatics of the Reformed Church*, the well-known collection of quotations from the orthodox Reformed theology of that time, was made an integral part of his own system.

b. Like the old Scholastics, he found it necessary to draw ever finer distinctions to satisfy the requirements of the intellect, so that the volumes of his *Church Dogmatics* continually swelled in bulk, and became a gigantic work comparable in size to one of the medieval *Summae.*

c. He traveled ever farther from his starting point, the "Swabian Fathers" of whom I have spoken, especially the two Blumhardts. The thing common to them was the fact that their faith did not rest upon doctrine, but upon the Word of God understood in its unity with Biblical history, and, secondly, that they saw in the God of the Bible the transforming power of life, and that because this transformation had come to a halt since apostolic times, they hoped above everything for a new outpouring of the Holy Spirit, and the promised consummation of the rule of God. There is hardly a trace of this hope left in Karl Barth. Just as significant is his increasing alienation from Kierkegaard's existential and dynamic view of apostolic faith, and from his searing criticism of "Christianity." For the Karl Barth of the *Church Dogmatics,* all this was pietism, a declension from pure doctrine.

This drift toward a new orthodoxy finds perhaps its clearest expression in the fact that Barth began to speak about "theological existence," and published a series of pamphlets under this general title. Nothing indicates more clearly his loss of his earlier insight — learned from Kierkegaard — that *faith* is an existence than this absurd connection of existence with *theology*. There is indeed such a thing as believing, or Christian existence, but no such thing as theological existence. For theology is reflection about faith, but not the life of faith. Once again, as in the age of Scholasticism, we are confronted with a theologism that is blind to the fundamental insight of the Reformers concerning the universal priesthood of believers, and that is in danger of turning upside down Christ's word about the "babes to whom the mysteries of heaven are revealed" (Matt. 11:25). At least Barth has never succeeded in distinguishing — indeed, he has never made a serious attempt clearly to distinguish — between belief in the sense used in his theology and the belief of nontheologians, the so-called laymen, who for all that, form the Christian congregation, i.e., between faith and reflection about the faith. The *objectum fidei*, the "object of faith," exercised so great a fascination upon him that he had neither interest in, nor understanding of, the identity of subject and object in faith, which was for the Reformers the very central doctrine of Christian faith. How could he when, for him, faith is only "the subjective realization of an objective *res*" (K.D. IV, 1, 828), of which it holds good that "faith only finds what is already there both for the believing and the unbelieving man" (p. 829)? Alongside of faith thus understood, neither love nor hope, which in the New Testament writers are bound in a unity with faith and are of the same importance, can get a fair deal. The unity of faith, love, and hope, which is the special theme of I Cor., ch. 13, but the general theme of the apostolic preaching, has never been made the theme of Barth's teaching. He has never felt the need of reflecting about the mystery of *this* triad, which is the mystery of Christian existence, while, neglecting the warning of the Reformers, he gave hundreds of pages to the mystery of the Trinity.

But if we inquire about the real, deepest reason for this later declension from the standpoint of the original Barthian theology, we must see it in an objectivism that was just as far away from the center of the Biblical faith of the Reformers as the subjectivism of the theology of a Schleiermacher, which Barth attacks. While it was precisely the decisive insight of the Reformers that all discourse about God was the discourse of faith, and that therefore a thought about the Trinity and election which bypassed faith, i.e., without a continual bearing in mind that our thought is an exposition of faith, would lead into the *merae tenebrae rationis,* and that consequently only the knowledge about God given us by faith has any importance for us — in Barth this correlation between God and faith is broken. The insight of Luther, that "God and faith belong together," is lost, and accordingly Barth does not deal with faith until near the end of his *Dogmatics,* and makes it clear there that faith has a very subordinate place in comparison with the revelation of God. Here we have certainly the antipodes of Schleiermacher's *The Christian Faith,* but this antipodes is just as far from the Biblical witness to God and Christ, which is always a witness of faith, as Schleiermacher. The correlation of the truth of revelation and the truth of faith that we find in the Bible and the Reformers is shattered, and the place of a divine truth that discloses itself only to faith is taken by a metaphysical speculation about God.

This transformation was indeed accomplished with a tremendous output of creative imagination and thought, and an astonishing expenditure of energy, so that this eruption of theological production for the moment simply took away the breath of Barth's contemporaries, and made every critical discussion impossible. This situation was all the more accentuated because the time of the development of this gigantic theological system partly coincided with the rise of the Hitlerian total state, in conflict with which Barth distinguished himself as the spiritual leader of the opposition, and won himself great moral credit thereby, not only in Germany but throughout the whole world. But with the end of the World War the time of theological stupor came to an end, and theological criticism, which had been mounting secretly, was able to find an outlet, free from the pressure of political threats. The counterstroke followed with a radicalism characteristic of the German people, a radicalism that tends to swing from one extreme to another. The extreme objectivism of the theology of Barth was followed by the equally extreme subjectivism of the theology of Rudolf Bultmann. Like Barth, Bultmann bypasses truth as encounter, only in the opposite direction, since his theology could speak only of faith, and had lost touch with the historical revelation, with God and his self-communication in his Act and Word, Jesus Christ.

Rudolf Bultmann is primarily a critical historian. In his *Theology of the New Testament* he sets himself the task of representing without prejudice the kerygma of the Christian community as the witness to Jesus Christ, and at the same time doing justice to the sources in their self-understanding. In so doing, he confronts the fact that this witness to Jesus, the Christ, the *Kyrios* and Savior, is not uniform, but on the contrary most diverse and not to be brought to one denominator. The Synoptic witness to Christ is one thing, Paul's another, and John's yet another. The task of the historian is to grasp each of these witnesses in its particularity, and here Bultmann in his above-mentioned *Theology of the New Testament* has to a large measure been successful. But he by no means considers that with this his task is completed. As a historian two things thrust themselves on his attention. All these characteristically different witnesses are designed for the sole purpose of bearing witness to the one, Jesus the Christ, and to him as the revealer of divine truth, and to him as the one who makes the life of believers new. To bear witness to him is thus at the same time to bear witness to oneself, as a man created anew through him. The intention of these writings of the New Testament is not to give the picture of a life, a biography; this biographical interest in the "life of Jesus" is quite alien to them. These men's intention is to speak of him as the one who has saved them, and indeed this aim is common to all of them, to the Synoptic writers as well as to Paul and John. They are concerned with the kerygma about Jesus, the Christ, with what they have to proclaim of him as the Savior of "every creature." *Hoc est Christum cognoscere, beneficia eius cognoscere.* This word of

46

the young Melanchthon [32] describes exactly what is the intention of the kerygma of the New Testament. To bear witness to Jesus Christ means thus at the same time to bear witness to the new life, the resurrection life of believers, to faith in Christ as the new life.

But now at this point Bultmann takes the fatal step of simply identifying this faith in Christ with the (new) self-understanding. Granted, faith *is* a (new) self-understanding. But two qualifications are here necessary: first, faith is a new self-understanding on the basis of the divine self-communication. Secondly, faith is not merely a self-understanding. It has also other quite different aspects of equal importance. It is in the first place a new relation to God, and the concept of "understanding" is quite unable to do full justice to its New Testament meaning. It is, above all, power and life; it is a transformation of the person, or rather the creation of the true person, the loving, responsible person in fellowship, the creation of the ecclesia. The reduction of faith to understanding brings about a transformation that reduces faith to something merely individual, something merely subjective, after the manner of idealism. Precisely that *extra nos* (Luther), that insertion into the Christ history, is lost which, in faithfulness to the texts, received its due emphasis in Bultmann's New Testament theology.

In addition to this, something else happened that led Bultmann's theology down the wrong road, its close connection with the existential philosophy of Martin Heidegger, the danger of which was pointed out to Bultmann as early as 1931.[33] In this way his theology was taken in tow by a philosophy — and what a philosophy! [34]

[32] *Loci Theologici* of 1521.
[33] Cf. Emil Brunner, "Theologie und Ontologie, oder die Theologie am Scheidewege" ("Theology and Ontology, or Theology at the Crossroads"), in *Zeitschrift für Theologie und Kirche, Neue Folge* 12, 1931, No. 2.
[34] Cf. Guido Schneeberger, *Nachlese zu Heidegger, Dokumente zu seinem Leben und Denken*, Bern, 1962 (*Gleanings from Heidegger, Documents Concerning His Life and Thought*), a collection of documents that throw a very sinister light on the figure of Heidegger

Bultmann has indeed always asserted that in the philosophy of Heidegger, this "fundamental ontology" is related to his theology as a mere presupposition, since every existential self-understanding presupposes an initial understanding, a knowledge about understanding in general. However correct this may be in a strictly formal sense, it was a disastrous error to suppose that Heidegger's ontology would be regarded as such a formal affair and placed at the service of the understanding of faith. Bultmann tremendously underestimated the potency of Heidegger's philosophy, and failed to recognize its incompatibility with what the Bible understands as faith. The "being" that Heidegger envisages is, in fact, on the one side, the same entity that Greek philosophy had in view, and at the same time the "nothingness" of nihilism. In this adoption by Bultmann of the ontology of his colleague of that time in Marburg, something happened that had already happened several times in the history of theology, the dovetailing of the Christian faith into a philosophy, and its subordination to that philosophy: this time, as a hundred years earlier, a philosophy of history, as becomes apparent in Bultmann's newest work, *History and Eschatology*.

From this connection of theology with philosophy there followed for him the double postulate of "demythologizing" and the "existential interpretation." [35] The former is certainly nothing new, but has been a powerful motif in theology since Origen, which cannot be denied a certain, though limited, justification. But it was bound, especially in connection with the second postulate, to lead to the stripping of the theology of Christ of its genuinely eschatological fundamental features, and surreptitiously to make it into an idealistic philosophy with strong nihilistic traits. "Being unto death" stands in irreconcilable op-

as National Socialist Rector of the University of Freiburg, and as a disciple of Husserl, to whom he had dedicated his *Sein und Zeit* in words of grateful discipleship, and whom he later defamed and persecuted as a Jew.

[35] Cf. my *Dogmatics* II, Appendix, pp. 311 ff. (E. T., pp. 263 ff.), "The Problem of 'De-mythologizing' (*Entmythologisierung*) the Message of the New Testament."

position to Christian faith as a " being unto (true eternal) life."

Certainly, theology can learn not a little from Heidegger. But the mere fact that Heidegger himself became suspicious of his *Being and Time* and never wrote the second volume promised by him, as well as the other fact that alongside of Heidegger's existential philosophy that of Karl Jaspers and, most influential of all, that of Jean-Paul Sartre came into existence, should have warned Bultmann not to make too close a connection with Heidegger. We should, rather, take note of the fact that there are several mutually conflicting systems of existentialism, among them the Christian system of a Gabriel Marcel. The connection of theology with philosophy has never yet been to the advantage of the former, neither the connection with Aristotle, Plato, or Plotinus, nor that with Descartes, Spinoza, Kant, or Hegel. Theology should be ready to learn from philosophy, but should be conscious that it draws its sustenance from another source. What resulted from Bultmann's connection with Heidegger was a mutilation, not an interpretation, of the New Testament witness to Jesus Christ.

Truth as encounter, on the other hand, points to the God who speaks to us in the Bible, above all, in the history of Jesus Christ. This Christ is neither the Christ of orthodoxy, nor the " historical [*historische*] Jesus " of liberalism, but the historic (*geschichtliche*) Jesus, the Christ and Savior of the Biblical message. Much in the Biblical picture of Jesus has not stood the test of historical criticism. But he himself speaks to us in this Biblical tradition with as much power today as before the beginning of Biblical criticism. In confrontation with the Bible, now as before, there happens " truth as encounter." In the Bible there encounters us now as formerly the truth of the God who came, is present, and will come to man. Faith is kindled, not by theology, but by the Word of God, by the history of the God who proclaims himself, and gives us a part with himself, and by the history of the Christ in the Old Testament and the New. The theologian, on the other hand, as the *verbi divini minister*, remains the servant of that which is given to him in the faith of the fellowship. Seen from this perspective, the conflicts of the

49

theological schools, which at first sight seem so tremendously important, are but insignificant episodes. They must be worked through, but the fact remains that in the Bible, truth as encounter still occurs as formerly it did, an encounter that changes the man who opens himself to it; in respect of his faith, making him to depend on God and to belong to God; in respect of his love, bringing him into the presence of God; and in respect of his hope, promising its consummation.

2. THE IDEA AND JUSTIFICATION OF A CHRISTIAN PHILOSOPHY

a. Although since the beginning of Scholasticism the Catholic Church has always acknowledged and given expression to the duality of Christian philosophy and theology, since the Reformation this duality has to a large extent turned into a conflict, which arose from a false concept of reason. This conflict has done much damage to the Protestant Evangelical Church, by leading, on the one hand, especially since the Enlightenment, to an ominous isolation of the church, and, on the other hand, to an unwholesome tutelage of culture at the hands of the church, which led to a theological imperialism — even though it was never able to enforce its claims. This " imperialism " has found expression in a certain domineering school of thought in German evangelical theology in recent times, and also, unfortunately, within the ecumenical movement since its institutional centralization. The isolation consisted in the separation of wide fields of scholarly research, especially in the human sciences, from the Christian faith, so that they remained unillumined by it, whereas this fatal cleavage did not occur in the lands of the Catholic Church, since Christian philosophy with its distinguished achievements was in the field. What is meant by Christian philosophy? What should we understand by this term?

We would do well to speak first not of Christian philosophy but of the philosophical work of Christian believers. Just as there are Christian artists, i.e., believing men who practice their art, so there are men who as Christians follow their calling as thinkers, just as, according to the Reformers' principle of the

50

universal priesthood, every man should express his Christian faith in his calling. Thus the man whose calling and task is thinking and philosophical activity should give expression to his Christian faith in his calling, and do what he does and must do to the honor of his Lord. The Christianity of such thinkers will manifest itself quite involuntarily, so to speak, in their thinking, and without describing itself as Christian. This was not regarded as self-contradictory and impossible until our age of positivism, when philosophy came to be regarded as autonomous and without presuppositions. But the thought of the absolute autonomy of reason is an illegitimate, most unfortunate prejudice, which achieved the status of an axiom at a certain period in the history of thought, whereas the philosophy of earlier times never lost its awareness of the limitations of human reason. It was the same prejudice that underlay the rationalism of the Enlightenment, a way of thinking that is infected with the sickness of detachment or emancipation from its origin, and is therefore essentially false thinking. This error has become continually clearer in the course of the last two centuries, and has at last come to its end in the self-contradictions of nihilism. On the other hand, this emancipation from theology's concept of God was not only understandable but necessary, inasmuch as theology was encumbered by dogma, and so to a large extent bereft of the freedom of thought. But if we understand Christian faith as an encounter of the divine Self with the human self, then all heteronomy and unfreedom is submerged in the theonomy of the new self-understanding, and thinking proceeds in the freedom of the Spirit.

To do philosophical work as a Christian is not the same thing as to do theological work. Theology is systematic preoccupation with the divine revelation of the Bible, whereas Christian philosophy is the reflection of a believing Christian about being and about existing realities as these are disclosed in experience of the world. It is reflection concerning the principles of being and of thought about being. But it is a thinking that is freed from the illusory prejudice of autonomy, because it knows of its own origin in the Spirit and will of the Creator, and in this

51

thought, which stems not from man's own resources but from God's self-communication, it recognizes and exercises its freedom as given, and therefore as a power with limitations.

Thus theology and philosophy are different from each other in respect to their subject matter, but are mutually complementary, not mutually contradictory. From the standpoint of the Christian, not philosophy, but *theology* is the first and most important, because by drawing from the Word of God in the Bible it throws light upon his existence as a Christian. But from the standpoint of being and thought in general, Christian *philosophy* is the first and most fundamental thing, because it thinks systematically the principles of being and of thought, freed from the false axiom of autonomy. Neither is philosophy "the handmaid of theology" as Thomas Aquinas believed, nor is theology dependent on "propositions borrowed from philosophy" as Schleiermacher conceived. Both have the same origin, but each has its different task of thought. Each is called to its special service. The "calling" of the philosopher is just as little holy as that of the theologian, but both of them are sanctified by the mandate of their common Master.

The highest objects of thought are being and thought about being. But the God of the Biblical revelation is neither that which is thought, the absolute object, nor the act of thinking, the thinking subject, but the self-revealing and self-communicating Lord of being. This was what Pascal meant by the words of his will, which was found sewn into his coat at his death: "*Dieu d'Abraham, Dieu d'Isaac, Dieu de Jacob, non des philosophes et des savants.*" What is meant is the living God who is not at the disposal of human thought, but who comes to man as the truth by making himself present, and makes himself known to man in his deeds, which are his words, and in his words which are his deeds. This God it is, who revealed himself to Moses in the words "I am that I am" (Ex. 3:14), in the word which the Neoplatonic Christian tradition has so often identified with the *ontōs on*, with the Absolute Being of philosophical speculation. The neutral impersonal or transcendent existent which is the highest, most abstract thought of philosophical speculation, has nothing to do with the "living God"

52

of faith, but during the early and late Middle Ages, during the Renaissance and in post-Reformation times, it had the profoundest influence on Christian thought, and is influential still today in the abstract concept of the *summum bonum, summum ens,* which is identified with the being of God. The first task of Christian philosophy consists in showing that the concept of the divine Being has nothing to do with this ontology of the *summum bonum,* but excludes it in principle. The true ontology is rather that of the absolutely free, self-determining will, which is determined by nothing but its own willing. Human creaturely freedom is based on this divine freedom as its origin. This human freedom knows itself called into being by this origin, and must determine itself in correspondence with this origin. Human existence is at the same time a being for freedom, and responsible being.

In contrast with the idealistic concept of freedom, that of Christian philosophy is not the concept of absolute unconditional freedom but of limited freedom. It is not the freedom of a self-dependent, but of a " dependent " being, whose ground and destiny is not in itself, but in the Will of absolute freedom, which is its origin and its goal. At the same time this fundamental character of human freedom is the source of its place of privilege among all beings, because it is man alone who hears that Word which calls him into existence. Even if the knowledge of the " history of nature " (Weizsäcker) shows that thousands of millions of years with millions of species of living beings have preceded the temporal appearance of man, this knowledge also indicates that all these living beings were forerunners of man, for in them nature was preparing the psychophysical form of man. It is indeed man alone who knows this, and in whose being, so long prepared, the leap into humanity was first made, whose center is " responsive actuality," re-sponsible freedom. The " answerability," the " re-sponsibility " [36] corresponds to the Creator's Word of summons. The freedom of man is

[36] TRANSLATOR'S NOTE: An untranslatable wordplay is given in the German. The two words " *Ant-wortlichkeit* " and " *Ver-Ant-wortlichkeit* " being divided thus, show the " over-againstness " of man to God, which is thus doubly indicated.

founded on this Word of summons, that calls him to the Creator, and makes him responsible. It is only in him that the plan of creation is realized. But we should not speak of " the person " of man in the singular only. Man is fundamentally distinguished from the Creator by the fact that he is found existing in an immense number of individuals, and that he can only realize his freedom in that fellowship in which every individual, whatever his peculiarity, has the same origin and the same goal.

Within the limits set by these fundamental alignments Christian philosophy and theology constantly interpenetrate one another. They separate at the point where what is thought of in the Logos of God comes into contradiction with God's will and with itself. This contradiction, its results, and its removal in temporal historical happenings, is not the theme of philosophy, but of theology as reflection about history in the light of its center, in the light of the re-stitution, the re-capitulation, and re-conciliation in the renewed gift of the incarnate Logos Jesus Christ, who has come to us, is present, and will come to us. Christian philosophy, however, seeks for that Logos, as it is to be found even in contradictory sinful personal existence, in the wide fields of human existence, in man's language, in his free creativity, in his cultural achievement, in his forms of fellowship, in his law, and in his state.

It seems in fact that the idea of a Christian philosophy could be made ridiculous by starting, as Bréhier does, from mathematics or physics, and asserting, " *On ne peut pas plus parler d'une philosophie chrétienne que d'une mathématique ou d'une physique chrétiennes.* " [37] But the question takes on a quite different appearance if instead we start with the concept of freedom, of personality, or of society, since there undoubtedly the Christian idea is distinguishable from every other idea. The question whether there is a Christian philosophy or not is accordingly not to be answered with " Yes " or " No," but only by the enunciation of a proportional proposition, which runs thus: The nearer a field of inquiry lies to that center of existence

[37] Quoted in Gilson, *De l'Esprit de la Philosophie Mediaevale*, I, p. 321.

54

where everything is at stake, i.e., where we have to do with the relation to God and the being of persons, the more clearly is the Christian viewpoint distinguished from every other one, while the antithesis between Christian and non-Christian becomes the more indistinct the farther the object of knowledge is distant from the personal center. Between the two poles of the personal center and mathematical physics lie the objects which do not indeed belong to the personal center but which stand in a certain greater or lesser proximity to personal being, as, for example, the family on the one hand, and the "impersonal" questions that are the theme of political economy on the other. Where the person in its relation to God is in question, the difference becomes an antithesis, but where on the other hand things are in the foreground, this difference diminishes to vanishing point.

Disregard of the "law of closeness of relation"[38] has been the cause of much confusion and unnecessary dispute, in that some have wished to subordinate everything to the Christological principle, and others nothing. It is especially within that Protestant Christianity which has no place for a Christian philosophy that this all-or-nothing attitude prevails, in which the "all" for the most part has remained an empty postulate, seeing that hitherto no theologian has succeeded in saying in what way Christian mathematics might be different from non-Christian mathematics. This controversy shows itself also in the so-called problem of secularism, which since the Reformation has been a crux of Western history. The whole intellectual history of the West illustrates an aspect of this problem, the increasing movement away from the personal center whose foundation is in God, and the corresponding phenomenon in the sociological field, the increasing depersonalization of man and the creation of a mass society that results from this spiritual fact and is to be explained by it. But with this our reflections on the idea of a

[38] Cf. my *Offenbarung und Vernunft*, ch. 25, " Problem und Idee einer Christlichen Philosophie," where on pp. 416–417 this law of closeness of relation was for the first time formulated, established, and explained. (E. T., *Revelation and Reason*, p. 383.)

Christian philosophy return to the theme of this Introduction.

b. But Christian philosophy is not only an idea and a postulate; it is a solid historical reality that is rather concealed than given its due place by such a title as *Towards a Christian Philosophy* (Hodgson). The eight volumes of Heinrich Ritter's *History of Christian Philosophy* give us only a faint reminder of the fact that it is just as difficult to " think away " the Christian element from Western philosophy as to " think it away " from Western history in general. We recall further the fact that it was only through Christianity that history itself ever became the theme of philosophical thought.[39] Whether this was an advantage for historical knowledge and for history as a scholarly discipline is a question to which eminent historical writers such as Jacob Burckhardt or Leopold von Ranke — with Hegel's philosophy of history in mind — have emphatically answered in the negative. As Christians we will have to come to a similar conclusion if we think of the beginnings of Christian philosophy in Clement of Alexandria and Origen, and the " apologists " who preceded them. But on the other hand, Augustine in his great work *The City of God,* and in his thoughts on the riddle of time in his *Confessions,* and in his utterances about human personality in his chief theological work *On the Trinity,* develops philosophical concepts that were unknown to ancient philosophy but which are indispensable to it today. Since Augustine was the first to reflect as a Christian on fundamental problems of philosophy, we cannot be too severe in our criticism of him because he was not able to set himself free from a synthesis of Neoplatonic and Christian ontology. Unfortunately, it was not he who chiefly dominated the thought of the Christian philosophy of the Middle Ages but the pseudonymous author of almost pure Neoplatonic writings, Dionysius the Areopagite, who was thought to be Paul's pupil. He is the most frequently quoted authority in the Middle Ages, and had almost as high a reputation as the canon of Scripture. It says much for the critical and philosophical insight of Martin Luther that he clearly recog-

[39] See above, Note 17.

56

nized the radically non-Christian character of the philosophy of the Areopagite, and warned men of it. It is also most probable that he recognized the pseudonym for what it was, a conclusion that later Catholic theologians proved correct, assigning to the Areopagite his historically correct place in the beginning of the sixth century instead of the first. Since then he has lost his pseudonymous authority also in the Christian philosophy of Catholicism, and the latter has remembered its genuine origins. It has again more decisively set its theological compass by the Bible, and has further developed its Christian philosophy in line with that of its true founder, Augustine. This is also the deepest reason why since then a more amicable conversation between Catholics and Protestants has become possible, and a mutual approximation has been initiated upon the common ecumenical theme. Since Augustine, Christian philosophy has repeatedly had notable exponents, sometimes even men of the first rank, both Catholic and Protestant. On the Catholic side there must be mentioned the mathematical genius and physicist Blaise Pascal, who was influenced by the Augustinianism of a Jansenius, and who by his *Pensées* both in his own day and today has liberated countless men of his own and modern times from agnosticism and atheism and brought them back to faith in Christ. On the Protestant side, the universal genius Leibniz must be mentioned, who on the one hand was one of the founders of modern mathematics and physics, and on the other, a true Protestant believer in Christ, who was a passionate advocate of the reconciliation of the Protestant and Catholic Churches. That as a philosopher he was one of the forerunners of the Enlightenment is just as true as the other point, that before Nietzsche he very clearly saw the " total solar eclipse " [40] which must result from the rapid growth of atheism. To this company also belongs the greatest mathematician of modern times, Leonhard Euler, who in addition to his numberless mathematical works bore witness in a great number of theological writings to his evangelical Christian faith, certainly without gaining great in-

[40] Cf. the magnificent vision of Nietzsche in *Fröhliche Wissenschaft*, pp. 343 ff. (E.T., *Joyful Wisdom*, Allen & Unwin, London.)

fluence on the history of philosophy. The founders also of the modern doctrine of natural law, Hugo Grotius and John Locke, were at the same time philosophers and evangelical Christians versed in the Bible. In addition to their philosophical works, both of them wrote a number of exegetical works on the Bible, just as Locke's pupil, Jonathan Edwards, the greatest philosopher of America, was at the same time the most eminent revivalist preacher of New England.

It is with justice that the "Magus of the North," Johann Georg Hamann, is reckoned as a quite extraordinary figure. Apprehended as a young man by the Christian message, he became through his views about language and poetry the brilliant and gifted teacher of Herder and Goethe, one of the founders of the philosophy of language, of the comparative history of literature, and of an aesthetic that bears witness both to his critical genius and his genuinely Christian faith of a Lutheran stamp. In spite of the century that separates them, the great Dane Søren Kierkegaard, who was at the same time a Christian philosopher and a Lutheran preacher and theologian, can be described as his pupil. In his debate with Hegel he gave the sharpest formulation of the antithesis between Christian faith and idealistic philosophy. Through his formulation of the concept of existence he became the founder of the existential philosophy — a fact today only too easily forgotten — and also the sharpest critic of orthodox Christianity and the Lutheran Church of his country and his time. The synthesis of philosophical thought and Christian faith that he created in less than fifteen years in his output of well over twenty volumes would be hardly believable were it not manifest beyond question. Related to Pascal in many respects, he grips us less than the latter through the crystal clarity of his thought than by its passion, by which he carries his readers with him — a prophet and preacher of repentance apprehended by Christ, and at the same time one of the greatest thinkers of modern times, whose precisest thoughts are still today trembling with passion.

As contemporaries of Kierkegaard without knowing the great Dane, two French Swiss thinkers, Alexandre Vinet and his younger friend and adherent, Charles Secrétan, the first specially influenced by Pascal, the second taking Schelling's late work, the *Philosophy of Revelation,* as his point of departure, but departing from it more and more, developed a philosophy of freedom, both of them drawing inspiration from the same source, the truth that encountered them in Christ. Their pupils, Arnold Reymond and Pierre Thévenaz, each made independent and significant contributions to a Christian philosophy. This whole school unfortunately and unjustly has been almost ignored as a small minority group. The philosophers of their time hardly took notice of them, being dominated by positivism and the axiom of autonomous reason. The only exception was the mathematician-philosopher, Emile Boutroux, and Henry Bergson, whose attention Boutroux had drawn to them. Both these thinkers valued highly Secrétan's philosophy of freedom, and allowed themselves to be influenced by it. Something similar is true of the philosophy of prerevolutionary Russia, and of Nicolas Berdyaev, originally an adherent of revolutionary Marxism, who during his exile in France wrote important works of Christian philosophy, which were, however, ignored by the atheistic philosophy of his second home.

A further list of Christian philosophers could be adduced, both of Catholic and Protestant provenance: on the one side, Theodor Haecker, Romano Guardini, both pupils of Kierkegaard; the essayist Baron von Hügel; the historian and philosopher Edwyn Bevan; on the other side, Josiah Royce and A. E. Taylor, who, although both of them more or less committed to idealism, produced a Christian philosophy of significant importance. But above all we must mention the brothers Richard and Reinhold Niebuhr, the latter of whom attained a much greater influence in the Anglo-Saxon lands than any theologian. They are indeed counted as theologians, but are nevertheless Christian philosophers. The same must be said of the German-American Paul Tillich, whose star is only now beginning to shine in the whole world, now that he has given up his teaching activity on the score of age. And the same is true of the Swede Anders Nygren, whose magnificent book *Agape and Eros* belongs completely to Christian philosophy, not to theology, although as a good Lutheran he will not admit it. As a pupil of Kierkegaard and Hamann, Ferdinand Ebner developed his I–Thou philosophy in his book of eccentric genius *The Word and the Spiritual Realities*, while at the same time Martin Buber developed his philosophy of I–Thou and I–It from his Jewish-Chassidistic tradition.[41]

This sketchy survey may be concluded with a reference to two important contemporary philosophers of different kinds, who are united by their common confession of Jesus Christ: Gabriel Marcel and Heinrich Barth. In his penetrating analysis of personal being, Gabriel Marcel conjoins insights drawn from Pascal and Kierkegaard, and pursues the theme of the *grandeur* and the *misère* of man. From this position he attacks the dogmatic nihilistic existentialism of a Sartre, and with his eye on man's self-surrender to technology develops a truly horrifying empirical apocalyptic. Heinrich Barth, the brother of the more famous theologian Karl, is a pupil of Hermann Cohen. As an evangelical Christian, he has developed Cohen's " philosophy of the origin " in his works on Plato, Augustine, and above all, in his chief work, *Philosophy of the Phenomenal*, independently, and shunning the glare of the footlights, and purposes to do so still further.

[41] The author of the first book, which appeared in 1921, a year before Buber's *Ich und Du*, was born in 1882 in Wien-Neustadt, and was a teacher in Gablitz. He died as early as 1931, and was not able fully to embody and defend his fundamental insight as Martin Buber has done throughout a long life. One of the few who grasped its epoch-making significance was Karl Heim, whose attention I drew to Ebner. In his postscript to *Schriften über das dialogische Prinzip*, Martin Buber gives a short sketch of the history of I–Thou knowledge, and speaks incidentally of Ferdinand Ebner as one of its pioneers. " This book showed me, as no other book since has done, in places with an almost uncanny insight, that in this age of ours men of different kinds and traditions had committed themselves to the search for the buried treasure." On the other hand, he speaks in the same place of Feuerbach's concept of the Thou as " a pseudo-mystical construction, from which neither Feuerbach nor anyone since him has been able to draw any genuine profit."

It was fatal that Luther, who knew only the " Christian " philosophy of the Middle Ages determined by Aristotle, believed that it was necessary to set philosophy in general in opposition to Christian faith in God. Although precisely the heart of his Reformation was that he experienced and knew faith as encounter with Christ, he could not quite yet free himself from the fifteen-hundred-year-old tradition that understood faith as belief in dogma. This circumstance, which was influential especially in the territory of Lutheranism but to a much lesser degree in that of Calvinism, contributed not a little to that cultural isolation which recently, with much exaggeration, has been called the ghetto-existence of the Protestant Church. On the other hand, the absence of this barrier in Catholicism has made much easier the latter's penetration into the culture of mankind. However, it is not a side-glance at the Catholic sister-Church but the truly Biblical, original Reformation concept of Christian calling that is the basis of our plea for the idea of a Christian philosophy or, rather, for the resumption of the tradition that was interrupted by the rationalism of the Enlightenment and by scientific positivism.

Christian philosophy will do well not to describe itself as such, because it will be conscious that by so doing, it would create a false appearance and awaken a prejudice that it can only overcome by thorough penetrative work. It will have to prove its Christian character especially through its strictly unbiased approach, through its open-minded attitude to all experience, and above all through its freedom from the prejudices of the absolute autonomous reason, and it will be able to do so. This prejudice has led the thought of the West into the abyss of the nihilism that denies everything and respects nothing. Only " the truth shall make you free," the truth which we do not have at our disposal, but which comes to us. With this truth we shall deal in the following pages in a systematic theological manner, reproducing the lectures of 1937 without alteration.

PART TWO

Truth as Encounter

PART TWO

I

Objectivism and Subjectivism in the History of Christendom

WHENEVER an individual, a people, or an epoch ceases to take existence merely for granted, two questions at once arise: " What is truth? " and " How can we become possessed of the truth which thus is? " The problem — how thinking or knowing is related to being — which more than any other has engaged Western philosophy from its first beginnings down to the present time, is not based upon a misunderstanding as has recently been maintained; it springs necessarily from our very existence. The familiar experience that there may be conflicting opinions concerning the same matter of fact is enough to force upon us the distinction between an objective being and a subjective knowing of that being. Especially in the sphere of science, though by no means only there, the striving for " objectivity," for the greatest possible correspondence between " thinking " and " being," is rightly regarded as the one true ideal of the search after knowledge.

We are not concerned here with this general philosophical problem, but only with the relation between the " objective " and the " subjective " in Christian faith. The question is theological rather than philosophical, not only in regard to its subject matter but also, and equally, with reference to its presuppositions. We ask not as those who are primarily interested to know if and in what sense there is truth in the Christian faith, but rather as those who, being believing members of the church, have knowledge of divine truth through the revelation in Jesus Christ. Our question arises, as we are accustomed to say today,

65

from within the church, not from without, and is intended as a backward-looking inquiry on the part of believers into the source, the foundation, and the norm, of their faith — which can be no other than the Word of God become flesh in Jesus Christ.

As men who in him find the truth, we raise the question concerning the relation between the objective and the subjective in Christian faith. But first of all let me explain how I arrived at this statement of the problem and why we may expect it to yield instruction that is not only serviceable to the church but in the highest sense necessary to it.

1. The Three Roots of the Theological Task

The task of theology — I am thinking now only of dogmatic and not of historical or exegetical theology — is to attain clarity as to what the church has to proclaim, what the Christian has to believe, and what the practical consequences of this proclamation and this faith are for the church and its individual members. This clarity it seeks to attain by means of reflection upon the revelation of God as given us in the Bible. This entire theological task, if I rightly understand the matter, has three different roots in the life of the church: the exegetical, the didactic, and the polemic. The Christian community needs help in its use of the Bible, and that not only in interpreting single texts or passages, but also in grasping the interconnection, in relating the single concepts to the revelation in its entirety. Thus, for example, the Lutheran dogmatic grew out of Melanchthon's *Theological Common Places*, which in its turn was meant as a guide for the Bible reader. So also the church has from the first recognized the task of instructing its members in the chief contents of the history of revelation and Holy Scripture in a sort of short compendium or catechism. The main facts and truths that form the foundation of the Christian faith are to be selected as such out of the great wealth of thoughts and occurrences that are crowded into the Bible, and exhibited in a definite, understandable connection to each other. Since, however, there are those among the church's members who are alive to the thinking and problems of their time and cannot be satisfied

66

with the elementary lessons of the first instruction, there arises the second type of dogmatic theology, as it first took shape in Augustine's handbook and, in monumental form, in Calvin's *Institutes*. Finally, the church since its beginning has had to be on its guard against the corruption of its message by heretics within and opponents without; it has had to oppose false with true Biblical doctrine, proving it to be such from the Scriptures. Inasmuch as this necessary work could be accomplished only through reflection upon the connected whole, there grew out of this root the third type of dogmatic theology, somewhat as it took form in Zwingli's *Commentary on True and False Religion*. It cannot fail to be realized that from this third source of dogmatic theology have come the most powerful, if not always the purest, impulses. Theology therefore is not only (systematized) Bible interpretation, not only (broadened and deepened) instruction, but fundamentally also critical reflection and controversy.

Since heresy all too gladly uses the Bible for its own purposes, its true nature can be exposed only by discovering its basic presuppositions. This controversy and critical reflection therefore often result in the statement of questions and concepts that are strange to the simple believer and even to the Bible itself — as, for example, those of the doctrine of the Trinity or of the two natures of Christ, or the problem of the authority of Scripture and the authority of tradition. Such questions and concepts are at first rightly held suspect by the community of believers. Since thinking is easier for us than practical obedience in faith and love, the danger of willful speculative developments is always with us, and these lead all too readily and in unforeseen ways to transformations in the gospel. And, indeed, the willfulness of speculative theology, whose particular intellectual interests have led it ever farther from the essential Biblical message, has brought heavy losses to the church both in ancient and modern times. Hence, the mistrust of all ideas that are not derived directly from the Biblical world is readily understood and entirely justified.

Yet unfortunately it remains necessary to ask these questions which at first seem alien to the immediate interests of faith,

67

most especially at those points where the proclamation and present faith of the church have already been molded and transformed, even though unconsciously and in unnoticed ways, by categories of thought to which the Bible itself stands opposed. Such transformations are particularly dangerous and difficult to recognize when they concern, not merely single articles of doctrine, but the whole of it; when they affect, like the sign before an algebraic parenthesis or the constant factors in a physics formula, every single concept of faith. Very early in the history of the church, for example, the idea arose under the influence of Greek philosophy that the divine revelation in the Bible had to do with the communication of those doctrinal truths which were inaccessible by themselves to human reason; and correspondingly that faith consisted in holding these supernaturally revealed doctrines for truth. This Greek intellectualistic recasting of the understanding of revelation and faith has caused immeasurable damage in the church to the present day. Yet it can be detected only very indirectly when the approach is from the Biblical point of view, since the entire Bible was written by Hebrews — by men from whom this misunderstanding which runs through all Greek philosophy lay as far distant as it lay close to the Greeks. To track down such a presupposition — foreign, even contrary, to the Bible itself — is therefore as difficult as it is necessary: difficult because it cannot be discovered in a single article of doctrine but extends through the whole of it; necessary because it has alienated from its peculiar meaning the entirety of Christian doctrine. The " sickness," figuratively speaking, lies not in a localized abscess or in a deformed organ but, rather, in the corruption of the blood, which thus secretly spreads the corruption into all organs.

2. The Biblical Understanding of Truth and the Object-Subject Antithesis

A supposition of this kind — untested and for the most part unrecognized and unconscious — from earliest times has burdened the church's understanding of revealed truth and has determined its practice. I refer to the application of the antithesis between object and subject, between the objective truth of faith (Credo) and the subjective acceptance of faith (credo). At once it seemed possible to place under this general philosophic antithesis the correlation, authoritative for the Biblical message, between the Word of God and faith or between the act of God and the knowledge of faith. For is it not very obvious that the Word of God is what is objectively given, while faith is the subjective appropriation of what is given? Once one is convinced of the legitimacy of this coequalization, I dare say one can and must go farther, and in similar fashion set other objectivities, such as the church as institution, the sacraments, or the offices, in contradistinction to the faith of the individual, and likewise confuse the superindividual-collective and the individual-personal with the antithesis between objective and subjective. Questioning these tradition-hallowed forms of thought will doubtless be neither easy nor without danger, since as a rule the greatest controversies, like the most serious errors, occur where attention is focused on such unverified suppositions, which are considered self-evident.

In order to be clear from the start about the subject matter of these chapters, I am already indicating the *thesis*, which is to be further explained and justified: *that the use of the objective-subject antithesis in understanding the truth of faith* and furthermore in the church generally is by no means self-evident; on the contrary, it *is a disastrous misunderstanding* which affects the entire content of Christian doctrine and also operates fatally in the practice of the church, most severely impairing the proclamation of the Word and faith among the fellowship. *The Biblical understanding of truth cannot be grasped through the object-subject antithesis: on the contrary, it is falsified through it.* This does not mean, to be sure, that we should avoid using this conception, since it is indispensable for natural-rational knowing, or that we can do without it in every respect; indeed we should have to stop thinking altogether if we entirely gave up using it. This thesis does mean, however, that where the heart of faith is concerned — the relation between God's Word and faith, between Christ and faith — the objective-subjective correlation must be replaced by one of an entirely different kind.

3. The Two Tendencies, Objectivism and Subjectivism, in the History of the Church

In order to clear the way toward an understanding of this thesis, I should like first of all to elucidate briefly several familiar facts in the history of the church, in which I must make use of the customary terminology, the pair of conceptions just questioned by me, namely, objective-subjective. Throughout the entire history of the church we see two tendencies, objectivism and subjectivism, competing with each other. Behind these two terms, which neither the Bible nor the simple believer recognizes, lie facts of the highest importance: errors in faith and in the church's transactions, corruption of Christian piety and sinful mistakes, which more than once have brought the Christian church to the very brink of misrepresentation and dissolution.

4. Two Kinds of Objectivism

Everyone who in some measure is gripped by the living Biblical faith as the Reformation revived it will be startled to discover the questions raised and answered in an authoritative textbook of Roman Catholic moral theology. For example, how long after it has been received does the consecrated Host of Christ remain in the stomach of believers? Shocked, we ask how such a misunderstanding of the holy meal instituted by our Lord could be possible. We may wonder less, though our astonishment will be no smaller, if we notice that in the same textbook appeal is made for decisions regarding all moral questions to the final authority of the Holy See; and obedient submission to it is inculcated as one of the chief duties of the Christian. Here, too, we recognize something wholly foreign to the Biblical kind of faith, an almost inconceivable change in the understanding of the obedience of faith. But these two and many other facts no less astonishing or weighty, at first seeming to stand alongside

70

each other without any connection, become understandable as symptoms of the selfsame " sickness " when considered from the point of view of objectivism. Both, in fact — this magical-materialistic conception of the Sacrament and this authoritarian concept of the obedience of faith, not to mention many other notions in the Roman Catholic theology and Church — have one and the same root, characterized by the catchword " objectivism." By " objectivism " I understand here a tendency of man's spirit and will to get something into his power — to manipulate it like an object in definite ways and within definite limits — something which by its very nature is not under human control. Man habitually exerts himself to build into a system of human assurances something of which he cannot dispose and which in essence is not disposable, such as divine grace and truth. Our Lord gave the Sacrament to his fellowship that in it he might be present to believers, thereby nourishing and strengthening their faith. Yet it was already misinterpreted and changed in the early days of the faith. A free gift of God, an event in which grace and the presence of grace in faith were freely bestowed, became a priestly sacrificial transaction whereby man received into his hand (so to say) the presence and grace of God. With the word of consecration the priest transforms the bread and wine into the body and blood of Christ, thus producing (as it were) salvation like a heavenly medicine — in the second century it was already called the medicine of immortality. Of course he is not allowed to effect the transformation miracle when and where he will, but he can do it *per nefas*. Salvation is in his — or at least in the church's — power. A practice wholly impersonal, something physical-metaphysical, has evolved out of an experience wholly personal, out of an event of the kind described by the words, " Where two or three are gathered together in my name, there am I in the midst of them." The Host is an object which the priest, or the church through the priest, produces by virtue of his office and by virtue of a mumbled word — " the transformation of the elements is not effected by means of the humble, solemn prayer invoking God's Spirit, but by means of the consecration formula spoken by the priest, who is

71

endowed with divine power" (Heiler, *Der Katholizismus,* p. 224). And the church disposes of this object just as it likes, in a way that has at the least a striking similarity to a material medicament. Hence, it is really considered an object. From this point of view the question and answer in the book of moral theology mentioned above, at first wholly incomprehensible to us, are understandable at least in their own context.

In the second case, the objectivism is of a subtler kind; but the fundamental point of view and tendency, and the process of transformation of the meaning of the Bible, are basically the same. It pleased God to make known to mankind the secret of his will in Jesus Christ, to reveal himself in the incarnate Word. But this revelation, although it was given once for all, remains God's right and God's deed, and hence reserved to himself alone. It is not and never can become something at man's disposal. The proclamation of the written word is God's Word, wherever and whenever it pleases him; the word of preaching is recognized as the Word of God only when and because the Holy Spirit gives it to be recognized as such. The human heart must be opened in faith through the power of God's own Spirit if that on which everything depends is to come to pass: the knowing of God. To be sure, the responsibility has been laid upon the church to proclaim to all the world the message entrusted to it; but it can manifest the Word of God only when that Word is especially given to it. The Word of God is no disposable object, but a free gift of grace. For "the Spirit bloweth where it listeth." The church "has" the Word, and yet it must always receive it anew, if it is actually to proclaim it. The preacher "has" his sermon, on paper or in his head; but it can become a mighty deliverance of God's Word only through the gift of God's Spirit — and for that he must constantly make renewed entreaty. This waiting and hoping, this dependence on God's free intervention, is always burdensome and vexing for man. If wholly dependent upon this free intervention of God, the church is most especially afraid in the life-and-death warfare that it must wage again and again. It would like to hold some assurances in its hand — who could not understand that! It

72

would like to have in its power for disposal that in which lies its stability and its very life. It would like to be certain of God in a more direct way than is guaranteed through the promise as given to faith and in prayer. So the church built up a mighty apparatus, a system of ecclesiastical assurances, by means of which it might become the power in control of the divine revelation. The authority of the divine Word was seized (so to speak) and made available in an ecclesiastical system of authority. The church of faith and the free-governing grace of God became the church of the holy episcopal canon law. The authority of the Word of God was delegated to this legal apparatus of the church, and the crown of this system of assurances is the papacy. When the pope speaks, God speaks: doctrine fixed by the Holy See is divine, revealed truth. *Roma locuta, causa finita* — Rome having spoken, the cause is decided. The erstwhile insecurity of the church has given way to an impressive, magnificent security, imposing to men of every age. Man now has what he wants. Now he has the divine revelation and also the secure human possession: the invisible and heavenly authority but also the visible and human. He has the Spirit of God and his gifts under his own administration and disposal; when he is ordained, the priest receives the Holy Spirit from the hand of the church.

What we have seen in these two especially clear examples from the ambit of Roman Catholic doctrine and practice will be observed during the course of this and the following chapters as obtaining within the whole sphere of the Christian church, in the Protestant no less than in the Catholic. Always and everywhere the same tendency to seek security rises out of man's sinful, anxious nature and therefore expresses itself wherever men have the church.

5. Subjectivism in the History of the Church

But this objectivism has its counterpart — if I may so express it — of equal rank: subjectivism — rooted as deeply in the being of man and just as devastating in its effect on the church. The striving for what is fixed, secure, authoritative, and disposable certainly does not hold an uncontested sovereignty; rivaling it is a drive at least as elemental and possibly even more primitive — the urge for freedom and spontaneity. Indeed, the development of systems of authority and assurances is partly a reaction against this unruly, fetter-smashing urge in the individual, which breaks through all fixed order in seeking to attain the highest possible unlimited self-realization. The urge for the adventure of freedom is fully as powerful as that for security, and Biblical doctrine brings it into especially close connection with the very essence of sin. Of this we shall speak in a later context. But the Word of God is first of all a taming of this insubordinate, egoistic desire for freedom. For it is concerned with establishing the sovereignty of God, with the obedience of faith, with the imprisoning of human reason by obedience to Christ, with validating the unconditional authority of God. The gospel came into the world as the obedience-commanding message of the dominion of God.

But the human heart with its egoistic desire for freedom asserts itself even here — where the gospel is accepted as well as where it is rejected. The First Letter of Paul to the Corinthians shows us how the Christian community from its beginnings had to hold off this false desire for freedom: individualistic enthusiasm [*Schwarmgeisterei*] is as old as the church itself. And *this* is subjectivism in the church. To defend itself against this subjective movement which would have undermined its very foundations, the early church built up a system of assurances. Primarily though not entirely, objectivism is a reaction to subjectivism.

In order to prove its ecclesiastical identity, objectivism clings to the historical givenness of the revelation, to the Word of truth given, spoken, and written once for all; the individualistic enthusiast, on the contrary, insists that everything depends on the free rule of the Spirit. " The Spirit bloweth where it listeth " — hence there is nothing fixed, nothing divinely given, no rule and authority, no established doctrine and institution. Nothing is binding but the free, ruling Spirit of God, who enlightens everyone, when and how He pleases. This enlightening through

74

the Spirit takes place, according to this point of view, from moment to moment, without established rules, without being bound to the fixed, given Word or to historical facts. Only the individual can experience it, and only in his solitary experience has he the certainty of the divine revelation. These individualistic enthusiasts have no other criterion or basis for faith than experiencing the impartation of the Spirit. All that is given and established, all fixed doctrine, all ordered office, all ecclesiastical constitution or arrangement — yes, even the fixing of God's Word in the Biblical canon — for them this is at once falsification, torpidity.

Throughout the entire history of the church movements have arisen in which this claim of the incommunicability of Spirit-enlightenment was defended against all ecclesiastical objectivities. The degree of subjectivism, that is, the radicalism with which this subjectivist principle of immediacy is asserted, varies very much, as does also the manner of its debate with objective church authority, its conjunction with, or open or secret opposition to, that authority. And correspondingly varied, too, is the reaction of the church. The history of the sects, the orders, mysticism, and the group movements of every kind, is filled with accounts of these times of reckoning, both inimical and peaceful. In fact, the changing relations between objectivism and subjectivism make up a large part of early, medieval, and modern church history.

6. THE DIALECTIC PRINCIPLE OF THE REFORMATION

From the Catholic point of view, determined by the objective idea of sacraments and church, the radical revival of Biblical faith that we call the Reformation must be criticized as subjectivism. In the following chapters I hope it will become clear why this reproach completely misses the mark. For the God-given power of the Reformation lies in the fact that through it the church was enabled to escape from this fatal antithesis, objectivism-subjectivism, and to find the secret of moving both between and beyond these extremes. Its " epistemological " principle was a dialectic; that is, its form of expression was never the use of one concept, but always two logically contradictory ones: the Word of God in the Bible and the witness of the Holy Spirit, but these understood and experienced, not as a duality, but as a unity. What is of concern is the truth given once for all, the truth of salvation and revelation clearly discoverable and available in the words of the Bible. But this Biblical truth can never be considered as available, willy-nilly, at the command of the church in doctrine or dogma, but as the Word of the living, present Spirit of God, wherewith the incarnate Word, Jesus Christ himself, takes possession of our hearts and himself makes his home there. This paradoxical unity of Word and Spirit, of historical revelation and God's contemporary presence, of " Christ for us " and " Christ in us " — this is the secret of the Reformation, of its power to renew Biblical faith and shake off the fetters of a century-long foreign rule, both theological and ecclesiastical. Time and again we are amazed to find, in dealing now with this, now with that, article of faith, that it is Luther who comprehends and brings fresh light: now in the doctrine of penance or of faith, of the church or the Word of God; now again at a quite unexpected point in regard to Greek intellectualism, sacramentalism, the holy canon law, the ecclesiastical legal doctrine; now in hidden Rationalism, individualism, the secret mystical haughtiness of egoistic enthusiasm. That he could so completely break through the errors of tradition to the fundamental ideas of the Bible always seems puzzling until we discover that it was the self-evident and necessary consequence of his freeing himself from the spell of a single false antithesis that determined the Catholic misunderstanding of the evangelical message as well as that of the individualistic enthusiast — the spell of the object-subject antithesis. This liberation enabled him to rediscover the original Biblical understanding of truth.

7. Objectivism in Orthodoxy

The church was given this liberating knowledge in its purity for all too short a time. The return to Catholic objectivism begins already at the close of the Reformation era itself, becoming more marked, however, in the age immediately after it. Even while controversialists were still arguing fiercely against the newly formulated Tridentine Catholic theology, they themselves had already unconsciously reverted in essential points to Catholicism. We call this the age of Protestant orthodoxy, and that phrase aptly characterizes the very essence of the period. Orthodoxy is one form — indeed the most important — of objectivism, and hence of objectivistic misunderstanding of the Biblical message. However anti-Catholic it may seem to be in the content of its faith or in its ecclesiastical postulates, orthodoxy is essentially Catholic because in it the Word of God is again made compassable; and the objective doctrine has become the actual object of faith. But we must not forget that in the age of orthodoxy as in the pre-Reformation era there existed alongside of or behind all orthodoxy a genuine, strong, and true Christian faith, such faith as produces " peace and joy in the Holy Spirit " and " which proves itself efficacious in love." The heritage from the Reformation was not simply lost. The consequences of the renewal of faith made themselves further felt in blessed ways — I need only remind you of the glorious treasury of church hymns, attaining a particular flowering time during this age, and above all of the courage with which the Protestant Churches and Christians under the cross stood their ground against the brutalities of the Counter-Reformation. And yet no one who studies the history of the post-Reformation period can escape the impression: a hoarfrost has fallen, a splendid growth has suddenly become as though cut off and benumbed. The age of orthodoxy appears like a frozen waterfall — mighty shapes of movement, but no movement. What happened? The paradoxical unity of Word and Spirit fell to pieces; the Scriptures became a gathering of divine oracles, the essence of divinely revealed doctrine. Men *have* God's Word. In the controversy against the Catholic principle of tradition on the one side and, on the other, the principle of the Spirit of the individualistic enthusiast, together with the newly arising rationalist principle, the temptation could not be withstood to create a system of assurances including the confessional dogma, the

77

notion of verbal inspiration, and the Bible understood as a book of revealed doctrine. The " paper pope " stands over against the pope in Rome; quite unnoticed, the position of dependence on the Word of God is usurped by the appeal to pure doctrine, which in turn is made tantamount to the Word of God. This displacement can already be noticed in a decisive way in the Augsburg Confession, even though still hidden by a living understanding of faith. Interest in doctrine more and more arrogates to itself every other interest; the urge for an ever-nicer precision in the formulation of conceptions — the absence of which in the whole Bible is so characteristic — becomes dominant in church life and leads to endless, even more subtle, doctrinal controversies. Christian love, practical discipleship, atrophies. Once let faith and recognition of a system of revealed doctrines become identical, and Christian piety, described in the Bible as " faith which proves efficacious in love," is seen in contradistinction to doctrine in the clearest and most definite way. Catechetical instruction becomes the preferred and practically the sole means of educating the younger generation to become Christians. The thoroughly trained Biblical theologian is the pattern by which the community should be directed for the understanding of its Christian life.

8. The Pietist Reaction

The reaction to this deterioration in the understanding of faith and in the church could not fail to appear. The counterstroke ensued, as is customary in history, *ex contrario*, in a movement not unjustly called Pietism, which carried in very various degrees the marks of subjectivism within itself. To be sure, the movement should be understood primarily as a renewed effort to make real the living, Biblical faith; and the appeal to Luther by some of its representatives has far more historical justification than is commonly recognized. Quite apart from its rejuvenation of the dried-up Protestant Church, what Pietism accomplished in the sphere of social amelioration and foreign missions is at least the token of that Spirit which is promised in the

78

Bible to those who truly believe, and is among the most splendid records of achievement to be found in church history.

That the movement seen as a whole likewise carried within itself the unmistakable features of a one-sided subjectivism, even as orthodoxy those of objectivism, is nonetheless indubitable. Albrecht Ritschl, despite the one-sidedness and mordancy of his judgment, is not incorrect when in Pietism he sees revived the old motives of the medieval Catholic mystic and of the individualistic enthusiast. The experience of the individual moves commandingly into the center of attention; pious feeling, even where theoretically this term was not used, becomes of chief importance. The hymns of that period clearly prove this contention, being a much more authoritative criterion than the theological assurances to the contrary. The comparatively trifling theological contribution of that epoch is also a distinct sign of the deficient understanding of the aim underlying the doctrinal controversies of the Reformation. Once again, as in the best periods of Catholic mysticism, the chief concern is for the sanctification of the individual, for achieving Christian personality wholly surrendered to God — by which is meant, in the idiom of Catholicism, the attainment of sainthood.

9. SCHLEIERMACHER

A point of view concerning which we shall have more to say later has recently directed attention, with some satisfaction, to the connection between Pietism and the rationalism of the Enlightenment. This connection is not to be denied; but if the picture of the situation is not to be falsified, it must at once be added that a similar causal connection also obtains between orthodoxy and this rationalism. Even as the Pietist subjectivism in certain extreme characteristics leads through the very heart of the " inner light " to the rationalist principle, so the extreme intellectualism of late orthodoxy directly prepares the way for the age of reason. In the figure of Schleiermacher the Pietism of his home background and the rationalist philosophy of his day are bound together in a remarkable personal " creative synthesis." Despite his vehement protests to the contrary, Schleiermacher is rooted solidly in the fundamentals of the Enlightenment. Like the rationalists, he searches behind the positive, historical religions for their common factor and for what at the same time would be for him their normative "essence," the "religion among the religions"; and he considers the Christian as the purest and most perfect form of religion. On the other hand, he is the confirmed opponent of the usual intellectualism of the Enlightenment and seeks the essence of religion in pious feeling. All revealed truth, in the last analysis, is submerged for him in this mystic feeling of unity over all antitheses. Subjectivism in Christian theology — that is, in the understanding of the Christian faith — enters with him upon a new phase. While most of the medieval mystics, and even more the Protestant Pietists, left the truth of the Word of the Bible unimpeachable and recognized its fundamental meaning for the church and faith, this can be said to be only seemingly true for Schleiermacher. His subjective interpretation of the faith of the church, when closely examined, tends to empty it of content completely. The Word is no longer the divine, revealed authority and the foundation of faith, but only the means of expressing that faith. What of truth-content remains in his "interpretation" of Christian dogma is hard to say. In any event this great thinker who understood how to bring together Pietism, the Enlightenment, and idealism into a most impressive unity, pointed the way to a distinctive feature of the nineteenth century — the subjective dissolution of theology.

10. Progressive Subjectivization

Despite the restraining reactions of the confessional orthodox and Biblicist schools of theology, the development of the understanding of faith during the last century on the Protestant basis unmistakably continued to move toward self-dissolution in the sense that it became more subjective. Even the emphasis of Albrecht Ritschl on the historical did not alter the situation, just because his concern was with the history of which man is

80

the subject, not God. The concern was not with God's revelation in his Word, but more and more with religion; not with the great facts of salvation in the Bible, but with "values" or with inner experiences or adventures; not with the event of redemption, but with the inner life of Jesus and the like; with factors that could be the objects of a religious psychology, possibly of a transcendental doctrine of the a priori, but not with the miracle of the Word of God becoming incarnate in Jesus Christ, the Mediator. It was reserved for the American "theology" in several of its schools of psychology of religion, however, to carry this tendency to a sort of ultimate extreme, so that in the Chicago school, for example, not much more was left of "religion" than a certain social feeling or value experience, for the truth-content of which it was wholly meaningless to ask. Even if Continental theology never went to such an extreme, a leading spirit such as Troeltsch was a warning sign that Protestantism was not very far distant from a skeptical self-dissolution.

11. Recent Theological Reflection and the New Objectivism

At this time the war broke out and swept away, together with so much that had become rotten, this hollowed-out, this empty theology. From various sides a powerful reaction set in. Luther was again remembered, and advance from him was made to a new understanding of justifying faith — an understanding born out of the need of the time. The Bible was again made the center for orientation; and, paradoxically enough, it was just out of the radical, final phase of the higher Biblical criticism, out of the results of the so-called eschatological school, that the entirely new impulse arose to take the Biblical message in earnest. The decisive opponent of the subjectivism of the past generation arose in the "dialectic theology." And finally, the understanding of the Biblical revelation, which, in spite of the prevailing trend of thought, the earlier Biblicist theologians had preserved or rediscovered, but which this trend had pre-

81

vented from obtaining due recognition, all at once produced unexpected results. Suddenly men like Kähler and Schlatter, hardly taken into account before the war, became recognized leaders. The theme of "religion" disappeared. People were allowed and wanted to hear again about the saving revelation of the Bible, of Jesus Christ, the Mediator of the divine covenant of grace. The age of subjectivism, at least in theology, was over and done with. The church as recipient and proclaimer of the Word of God was again taken seriously.

But when the church is taken seriously, its shadow also immediately appears again: objectivism. We have already seen that particularly during times of controversy, when the church as a whole must defend itself against a menacing power that threatens its very existence, the temptation becomes strong to imprison the Word of God in a system of human assurances. Men want to hold something solid in the hand with which to fight. In controversy, especially with strong forces from without, there is little time for critical self-interpretation. Massive formulas are needed. The opponent must be met on terms more or less even. The tendency to make political both the theological conceptions and the bearing of the church is clamant and, humanly speaking, entirely understandable. But the means used is orthodox theology, confessional orthodoxy. It is the product of the tendency toward security, the expression of the determination once for all to secure from every attack the essence of the church. The ready-made concepts of confessional orthodoxy are much better suited as weapons of attack and defense than the dialectically oscillating and organic-parabolic notions in the Bible itself. Quite unnoticed, a neoorthodox theology shapes itself out of the earlier dialectical theology, and it carries all the characteristic marks of objectivism: one-sided emphasis on doctrine, identification of doctrine with the Word of God, overvaluation of the formulated creed, of dogma; one-sided prominence given to the objective factor in preaching, the church being understood primarily in terms of doctrine, sacrament, and office, rather than as the fellowship of believers, the church being understood as institution; neglect of love in favor of orthodoxy, of practical discipleship in favor of a strict churchly attitude; misunderstanding of the missionary and pastoral task of the church as the result of a one-sided estimation of the sermon as the didactic expounding of the Bible, and so forth.

Perhaps it would be more correct to speak of this theological, ecclesiastical objectivism, not as being already present, but rather as in the process of becoming of considerable importance. In any event let us not speak down from any kind of safe bulwark to those who stand in a hard, brave battle and for that reason let themselves be pushed in this direction — thus spoiling the joy of the fighting with the cheap criticism of a spectator. On the contrary, we observe with joy that within the ranks of the bravest the demand for renewed reflection, the warning against overconfidence in the confessional formula, is making itself distinctly heard. But we should not forget that theological movements, once started, follow their own law and produce specific effects of their own even when quite separated from the original controversial situation. It is upon us who do not as yet have a part in this struggle with the beast out of the pit that the double duty is laid to use for very earnest reflection the respite allowed us, on the one hand, in order to be better able to help those who are in the combat, on the other, to prepare ourselves for the conflict that will also come to us, though probably in quite a different way. The defensive combat that is the brave defense of the gospel proclamation and the church clearly is not the only duty ordained for us. For we are summoned to proclaim the gospel to all creatures, to make disciples of all peoples. But orthodox theology has never yet had missionary power, nor created missionary impulse.

12. The Necessary Reminder About the Word of God

I hope it has become somewhat clear in this hurried historical sketch that the concern of our day is not to avoid the Scylla of an already existing orthodoxy only to give way to the Charybdis of a new Pietism. For the grave injustice that undoubtedly has been done Pietism during the past twenty years, I feel it a duty, as one of those more or less responsible, to make some amends. It is precisely we — the group of "dialectic" theologians who several years back still enjoyed some unity in being fellow combatants — who have every reason to remember Pietism with the highest gratitude. For the best that we had when we started we were indebted, humanly speaking, to two great figures of Pietism — Chr. Blumhardt, in Boll, and Kierkegaard, the man who, likewise in conflict against a false objectivism, ventured the daring sentence: Subjectivity is truth. But it is not and should not be for nothing that we also saw clearly the dubious aspects of Pietism, just this subjectivism; hence our watchword can be none other than: *Beyond orthodoxy and Pietism, Biblical faith!*

For this reason, it is the urgent imperative of the hour to search, by means of reflection about the Word of God itself, for this "beyond" of objectivism and subjectivism which is the secret of true Christian faith. Quite naturally the first thought is that the truth must lie somewhere in the middle, like the arithmetical mean between two extremes. The task for the exponent of objectivism as of subjectivism, according to this view, would be for each to help the other toward a true evaluation and thereby to a correct delimitation of his own position: this is the expedient of mediation. But one glance at history, specifically at the Reformation, makes this way appear like a feeble compromise which only obscures the real problem but does not solve it. There is no right middle way between objectivism and subjectivism: there is no correct mean between two errors. In this instance too the truth is more paradoxical and harder to find. It is not possible to plead the case too strongly for either the so-called objective or subjective element in faith. The more the one is stressed, the more valid the other becomes. But in actual fact the formula is false.

With this I come back to the thesis suggested at the beginning of this chapter. In any event the damage to the church did not lie in the one-sided emphasis on either the objective or the subjective but, rather, in the fact that the Biblical revelation was brought under this antithesis. The Bible is as little concerned with objective as with subjective truth. The objective-subjective antithesis cannot be applied to the Word of God and to faith. It is a category of thought wholly foreign, not only to the way of expression in the Bible, but also to the entire content. To remove it from the understanding of God's Word and faith is the purpose of these chapters. Through what has already been said I hope that I have indicated to some extent that this thesis is really significant and of importance for the church. Above all, however, I am anxious to show in the following chapters how through eliminating this tradition-hallowed but devastating prejudice, Biblical truth rises to a new splendor.

II

The Biblical Understanding of Truth

T HE SOURCE and norm of all Christian theology is the Bible. Its subject matter is the secret and, at the same time, manifest meaning of the Bible: the God who inclines himself toward man and makes himself present to man: Jesus Christ and his Kingdom. This is the presupposition (never to be lost from sight) for my attempt to work out the opposition between the Biblical understanding of truth and the general rational understanding of truth as determined by the object-subject antithesis. This understanding of truth is nowhere explained in the Bible. Even if we brought together and analyzed exegetically all the Biblical passages in which the word " truth " occurs, we should be hardly a step nearer our goal. Just as the Bible explicates no " principle of interpretation " and contains no " doctrine of the Word of God," so we search it in vain for a " doctrine of truth." The more formal a theological concept is, the less it can be directly discovered in, or directly validated by, the Bible itself. Formal theological concepts are attempts to lay hold of the hidden presuppositions, so to say, the structural form of the Biblical revelation. The passages in which the Bible speaks specifically of the Word of God are proportionately scarce; and yet everything in the Biblical revelation is determined by the category of the Word of God. God is the kind of God who reveals himself in the Word, even as he also creates and sustains the world through the Word. The task of theology is to elaborate what is formal and at the same time to place it in such a relation with the central contents of the Biblical revelation that it becomes clear how this structural " form " is determined by the " matter " and the " matter " by the " form." The God of the Bible is a God who speaks, and the Word of the Bible is the Word of this God. The " formal principle," the Word of God, and the " material principle," redemption through Jesus Christ or justification by faith alone, are not two but one and the same principle seen in two aspects. Similarly, in the following chapters what we hope to work out as the Biblical understanding of truth is not different from what is the concern of the Bible itself; and the formal nature of the concept " understanding of truth " and other similar concepts may not be understood as if they pointed to a priori, general epistemological or ontological categories interpreted into the Bible from outside. On the contrary, they are taken from nothing but Scripture itself and stand in the closest connection to all its central contents (as we shall see in later chapters). They are in fact none other than these very contents, considered in their formal aspect, which as such are never directly mentioned in the Biblical word.

The Biblical revelation in the Old and New Testaments deals with the relation of God to men and of men to God. It contains no doctrine of God as he is in himself [Gott-an-sich], none of man as he is in himself [Menschen-an-sich]. It always speaks of God as the God who approaches man [Gott-zum-Menschen-hin] and of man as the man who comes from God [Menschen-von-Gott-her]. That God — even in his " I-am-ness " [An-sich-sein] — wishes from the first to be understood as the God who approaches man is precisely the meaning of the doctrine of the Triune God; that man, even in his natural being, is always the man who comes from God is the meaning of the doctrine of the image of God and of original sin. And both are known in their fullness only in Jesus Christ, in whom as the incarnate Son of God both the God who approaches man and the man who comes from God are revealed.

This last suggestion leads naturally to another: that in the Bible this two-sided relation between God and man is not developed as doctrine but, rather, is set forth as happening in a story. The relation between God and man and between man

87

and God is not of such a kind that doctrine can adequately express it in abstract formulas, as it is possible to express abstractly, for instance, the relation between the radius and the circumference of a circle or the relation between the beautiful and the good. It is not a timeless or static relation, arising from the world of ideas — and only for such is doctrine an adequate form: rather, the relation is an event, and hence narration is the proper form to describe it. The decisive word form in the language of the Bible is not the substantive, as in Greek, but the verb, the word of action. The thought of the Bible is not substantival, neuter and abstract, but verbal, historical and personal. Its concern is not with a relation that exists in and for itself, but with a relation that (so to say) occurs. God " steps " into the world, into relation with men: he deals with them, for them, and in a certain sense also against them; but he acts always in relation *to them*, and he always *acts*.

Similarly, men are also considered as those who are not something in and for themselves, but only as those who from the first are placed in a specific relation to God and then also place themselves in such a relation: either positive or negative, obedient or disobedient, true or false, comformable to God or impious. They, too, are always considered as those who act: and their action, whether expressing sin or faith, is always understood as action in relation to God.

1. The God of Man and the Man of God

The God of the Bible is always the God of man, and for that reason is not less but more exalted than the God of the philosophers or mystics. He is never other than the God of man. That is to say, from the first he is that God who " hath in these latter days spoken unto us by the Son," in the incarnation of the Son of God; the God who is concerned about his sovereignty over and fellowship with man, so that whenever one thinks of God he thinks at the same time of his will for mankind. Similarly, *man in the Bible is always the man of God* — and therefore not less but much more human than the man of the philosophers.

88

He is never other than the man of God, even though he be also sinner, impious, or forsaken and repulsed by God. Even hell itself is only hell because it is hell in relation to God. What actually happens in this relation of God to man and of man to God makes up the content of the Bible.

But this relation, although two-sided, does not have equal or interchangeable terms. More correctly it is one-sided in that it originates with God. The initiative in this relationship is taken by God, and only in a secondary way does man have any initiative in it at all. The relation of God to man is always first, that of man to God second and consequent upon the first. Hence, the relation of God to man is wholly other than that of man to God. The relation of God to man is clearly primary, creative, and without presuppositions. The relation between God and man could not possibly be stipulated by any impulsion from the human side. God's relation to man has no sort of presupposition in a relation of man to God. On this point there is basic opposition between the Biblical and the idealist, pantheist, and mystical thought concerning God. Clearly, God is first. He paints his image of man on the canvas of nothingness, as it were: and there he stands, a man. God calls man into existence out of nothingness — even though in doing so He uses material which he has prepared previously. And, contrariwise, man's relation to God is secondary: it is consequent upon and determined by the already existing relation between God and man, established through no human effort. The relation between God and man is thus always reciprocal, yet never interchangeable like the relation between left and right. God is always and inconvertibly the first, man always and inconvertibly the second in this relation.

2. WHAT HAPPENS IN THE RELATION BETWEEN GOD AND MAN

The Bible teaches about this God and this man, and about this *indissoluble two-sided, yet never interchangeable and in a specific sense one-sided, relation between them.* God is known in his relation to man, we are told; and likewise, man comes to know himself in his relation with God. Three factors closely connected with what has already been said about this knowledge need to be pointed out. First is the way in which this knowing and being known finds expression: that the relation of man to God is secondary, not primary. That is, man can know God only as God gives himself to be known: this is the fundamental Biblical point of view. In a later connection we shall understand that the Bible even makes the further assertion that man can know God only because and insofar as he is known by God. To such a large extent emphasis is placed in the Bible upon the unconditional priority of God in the relation between God and man. The second factor is contained in the first: this knowing is therefore an event, an act. God gives himself to be known, he reveals himself, he communicates himself. On the basis of this revelatory happening or act, man can also know God and his relation to Him, which is itself established by God. Man, moreover, also gains this knowledge in an event, in an act of decision. The unconditional priority of God and the active nature of this knowing are linked together, as can be seen when contrasted with the idealist, mystical teaching. In this teaching, the priority of God, this unlikeness between the divine and human subject, does not obtain, but, rather, an emphasis on the interchangeability, so to say, of the two parties in the relation. Hence, knowledge is not an event but something timeless, a static capacity in which the actual emerges out of the potential by sheer chance. In the idealist-mystic teaching, knowledge is neither revelation nor decision, but a perception of something that was always " there," ready to be perceived.

The third factor is already indicated in the second: this revelation is itself the decisive element in the act of relation between God and man, is indissolubly connected with it. It is not true that first of all there is a relation between God and man, between man and God, which can be known even though it does not become actual. As a matter of fact, it is precisely in God's giving himself to be known and in this knowledge of God that the essence of the relation between God and man lies.

90

God meets men so vitally in this relation that they ought to know him. The revelation of God to men is the decisive element in what God does for them. And on the other hand, the knowledge of God is the decisive element in the relation to be realized between man and God. God is the God who approaches man just because and insofar as He reveals himself; and man is the man who comes from God because and insofar as he knows God on the basis of his revelation. God is always the One who destines man for, and calls man to, Himself; and man is always the one so destined and called by God. The event that is the relation between God and man hence is always an act of revelation: likewise, the event that is the relation between man and God is always a relation based on knowing. For this reason, the content of the Scriptures, as narration about this relation which is established from God manward and from man Godward, is always a history of revealing and knowing. Even the narration of the Bible itself is an integral element in this history, in which the relation of God manward and of man Godward is realized. Thus the narration of the Bible is not something to be added as ordinarily the story is added to the event — we think of the complaint of the epic singer that he could " only " tell what the heroes had actually " done." No, the Biblical narrative itself is a part of the history in which God makes actual his relation to man, in which his Kingdom is realized. It cannot be otherwise, for that which is most essential in the ultimate goal of this history, in the Kingdom of God, is the seeing of God face-to-face, that " knowing even as we are known."

3. GOD CREATES A COUNTERPART, FACE-TO-FACE WITH HIMSELF

It will be of value to examine even more closely this relation between God and man. First of all, we must note that God creates for himself a person as a counterpart of himself. This decisive affirmation we make in the sentence from the Apostles' Creed, " I believe in God the Father Almighty, Maker of heaven and earth "; we assert that God wants and creates and endows

91

an actual counterpart who therefore is not himself and yet who exists only because God so wills it. In this way Biblical faith in God is differentiated from all pantheism.

There are trends of thought in Biblical faith that seem to lead to the very edge of pantheism — for instance, the thought of the divine omnipotence, the all-efficiency, the all-determining decree, and the like. But the boundary is never crossed: the world and, above all, man stand " over against " God and can never be identified with him. God wills it thus himself, he has himself thus arranged it, and he would not change it through all eternity. He gives his creature being, face-to-face with himself — indeed, not an independent but a dependent-independent being. God endows the creature with the power to *be* " over against " him —indeed, the power to keep his own being face-to-face with Him.

To what extent this holds for subhuman nature it is hard to say, since we know it only from the outside. Nor is it of particular importance. In the Bible the subhuman creature (together with certain superhuman powers) is only frame and setting for what takes place between God and man. It has no right to an independent significance for reasons that are yet to be discussed. But the human creature is endowed by God with independent being. The dependence upon God of this creaturely being is, through God's ordinance, of such a kind that at the same time it is always freedom. God places himself face-to-face with a free being. Every form of determinism, any thinking whatsoever that questions or completely denies human freedom, is wholly foreign to the Old and New Testaments; and the fact of man's slavery to sin (of which I shall speak more fully later) should never have become confused with it. Determinism, through Augustine, having found its way into Reformation theology, has a Stoic and not a Biblical origin. The Bible speaks of only one relation between God and man, in which man by virtue of God's will and God's creation has a decisively free, independent being, not only toward other creatures, but even toward God himself. Hence, when one believes (as has often happened and is still happening in the field of Protestant theology) that to uphold the honor of God he must belittle man's independence and freedom or even defend determinism, he does not serve the God who has revealed himself to us in the Holy Scriptures but, rather, an abstract, philosophical idea of God. Why so much emphasis falls upon the human creature's independence, which stems from the Biblical idea of God, shall be indicated immediately.

But first of all let us note the other side. This independence of man is never independence from God; contrarily, man's freedom is grounded precisely in his dependence on God, so that a maximum of freedom is at the same time a maximum of dependence. Man is the more free, the more he is conscious of his dependence on God and the more dependent he makes himself; the less free, the more he denies this dependence and seeks to withdraw himself from it. Being and knowing are here inextricably intertwined in the manner of which we spoke a moment ago. But it is never true that apparent independence means actual independence. On the contrary. The very man who questions his dependence on God draws every breath by leave of the Creator whom he denies. True humanness and true freedom, however, both of which are lost by the man emancipated from God, are present only when man knows and acknowledges his complete dependence on God. Complete dependence on God is at the same time true freedom. In this way Christian thought is delimited from all deism, which stresses the autonomy of the creature in such a way as to destroy the very concept of creature. God places " over against " himself a real counterpart, a creature of such a nature that he can say no to God, but a creature who in the very act of saying no loses his true strength and freedom.

4. Lordship and Fellowship

The enduring basis for these assertions must become apparent as a result of more closely examining the nature of the relation between God and man. As yet we have considered this relation only formally, in order first of all to let its structure as such stand out in relief. But only when we have clothed this skeleton with the contents belonging to it can we recognize the message of the Bible in our train of thought. The relation between God and man, with which the Bible is always concerned and which in fact is the single theme in the entire Biblical proclamation, can be stated in two words: *Lordship* and *fellowship*. The pivotal point in the Bible is the concept " Kingdom of God," a dual notion holding within itself the ideas of God's being and becoming Lord over men and his fellowship with them; from beginning to end, from the first chapter of Genesis to the last chapter of Revelation, this is the pivotal point around which all turns. These two ideas of Lordship and fellowship must now be examined more carefully for their exact meaning. Through them we shall find determined the whole of Biblical doctrine, and with it what is our particular aim, the specific Biblical understanding of truth.

What do we mean when we say, " God is Lord "? First of all, simply that God can do what he wills with what he has created. Face-to-face with the Creator, the creature has no rights and no power that God has not lent to it. In the concept of Lordship the complete dependence of the creature thus finds a definite expression. To declare that God is Lord is basically nothing other than to take with entire seriousness the idea of creation. That God really is Creator means that the creature has neither right nor power that is not derived from God. This holds for every creature.

But something distinctive obtains for man that really first gives the concept " Lord " its complete Biblical meaning and its positive content. For the assertion that the creature has no right or power that does not come from God is first of all a negative designation. But God wills to be Lord not only " over " man: he wills to be Lord " of " man. God is Lord " over " clouds and winds, over plants and animals, over galaxies and over atoms. But God is not " their " Lord. That God is Lord of man means either that he *wills* to be known and acknowledged by man or that he *is* known and acknowledged by man as the One to whom man unconditionally belongs. Because God wills to

94

be and can be Lord only in this way, he places himself face-to-face with an independent creature. For only an independent creature can know and acknowledge. God wills to be acknowledged as Lord in freedom, since it is by virtue of such free acknowledgment that he is Lord in the highest sense. Because so much worth and stress is laid upon the Lordship of God in the Biblical revelation, so much stress must be placed in the Bible on the independence of man. The emphasis upon this independence hence has nothing to do with the freedom-of-the-will motif of Greek or modern humanism. It is, if I may so express it, a theocratic humanism.

God places a creature face to-face with himself, a creature who in having the power of knowing and acknowledging has a share in the essential nature of God, namely, in being a subject. Perhaps we shall also have to concede that in subhuman nature — but in a much weaker and more indistinct sense — there is something of the nature of being a subject; but in the sense of free knowing and acknowledging, in the sense of voluntary subordination of the creation under the Creator, man alone of all created beings known to us is suited to be a subject. Because the will to Lordship is inextricably linked with the nature of God (that nature as known to us in his revelation), God as we said right at the start is always the God who approaches man. And because this subjectivity of man is, according to the revelation of the Bible, exclusively grounded in God's will to Lordship, man is always the man who comes from God.

Perhaps it is possible to imagine a merely reflecting subjectivity, that is to say, a consciousness that is related to its counterpart like a mirror to its reflection. It is even possible to think that such a consciousness would reflect God's Lordship as a mirror reflects what stands before it. Indeed, we even possess in a certain sense this mirrorlike subjectivity, especially when we receive within ourselves impressions of objects in a completely uninterested way, involuntarily, and in entire passivity. With such a mirrorlike or echolike counterpart, God is not concerned, for thereby his will as Lord is not sufficiently exalted. In freedom, in free decision, in self-sacrifice, he wills to be known and acknowledged as Lord by his counterpart. He is concerned about the free obedience of his creatures. Because in the full sense God can be Lord only of such a subject who in free personal decision acknowledges him as Lord, he wills this independence of the creature in the very same unconditional way that he wills to be Lord. From this consideration we can see how fundamentally the God who reveals himself to us in the Bible is misunderstood if one believes that he must exalt the divine omnipotence and absoluteness at the cost of human freedom and independence. It is decisively Biblical that in the knowledge of God his omnipotence and absoluteness are maintained together with this freedom of his creaturely counterpart, and every attempt to deny this face-to-face relationship for the sake of a supposed exalting of the divine omnipotence will be rejected. Not the *Deus absolutus* — that "God" to which an abstract philosophical thinking leads — but the Lord our God, whose will it is to be Lord in a Kingdom of God, is the "God of Abraham, Isaac, and Jacob," the "Father of our Lord Jesus Christ." That the creature can be in freedom "over against" God is grounded in the will of God to be Lord, and man's unconditional interest in God is given with and grounded in his unconditional interest that God may be Lord.

This is the concrete meaning of our purely formal opening statement, that the Bible says nothing of a God as he is in himself and nothing of a man as he is in himself, but only of a God who from the first is related to man and of a man who from the first is related to God, and, indeed, in such a way that in this relation God is inconvertibly the first, man inconvertibly the second. We say now that God is the Creator-Lord and man is the creature, created to be freely obedient. The Biblical revelation of God shows us this and no other God, and God wills to be called by this and no other name: the Lord who in a freely obedient mankind wills to realize his Lordship, the God of the Kingdom of God. Nowhere is the Bible concerned with an abstract divine omnipotence and an abstract absolute. To be sure, no obliterating of the boundary, no equalization of any sort between God and man, is suggested when we say that the independent freedom of the human creature is to be maintained as unconditionally as the Lordship of God; for this free selfhood of man is grounded only in God's will and Creator-power, and his self-realization depends entirely on the acknowledgment of this absolute dependence on God's will and power. God alone is the source of man's being and freedom, and God's *will* and *creation* is indeed this source, not some eternal timeless emanation or essential interrelatedness. But as certainly and unconditionally as God wills to be Lord, so certainly and unconditionally he wills to have his free counterpart. Whoever therefore abandons this unambiguous but double-sided basic relation for the sake of an ostensibly higher, holier notion of God may be concerned about God's being taken more absolutely and more seriously. Actually, he is thus interpreting the omnipotence and all-efficiency of God as sole-efficiency and so canceling out the true face-to-face relation. In this way he veritably destroys the Biblical thought of God.

The second concept by which this formal two-sided relation is made concrete is that of *fellowship*. Above all and in a unique way God wills to have fellowship with his human creatures. This second concept presupposes the first; but the first is fulfilled only in the second. We have just said that God creates a counterpart who in freedom acknowledges him as Lord, but God does this that he may communicate himself to this creature in love. He wills his creature should not only acknowledge him as Lord and obey him, but that it should love him in return with that love which he himself bestows upon it. In this relation too, God intends to be unconditionally first. In contrast to all Platonic or Neoplatonic *erōs*, God's freely given love is first, man's love for God — always a reciprocated love — is second and is consequent upon the first. Similarly, man in loving is unconditionally dependent upon God. This love is completely grounded in God's will and act; but it is nonetheless the free, spontaneous love of the creature.

If God's will to Lordship is his *self-affirmation* " over against " and in the creature, then his love — his will to fellowship — is his unconditional *self-communication* to the creature. God as

Lord wills to be loved; obedient acknowledgment of the divine Lordship is the essential presupposition of love for God. But love for God cannot be grounded in his Lordship by itself, but only in such a kind of Lordship in which he communicates himself. Man can unconditionally love only the unconditionally loving God. The relation of the fulfilled condition thus subsists between Lordship and obedience on the one hand, and between self-communication and responding love on the other. This must be understood in greater detail.

First of all, it is clear that what was said about acknowledgment of God as Lord holds good especially for love: love presupposes complete freedom. Enforced love is not love at all. To be anything else except free contradicts the nature of love — precisely that love depicted in the Bible as the right kind of love. Love presupposes an even higher degree of freedom than the acknowledgment (in obedience) of God as Lord. Love is the most freely willed of any activity of which we are able to think. Love is actually the essence of free will, and contrariwise, the essence of free will is love. Hence, love is the very opposite of all involuntary, disinterested reflex subjectivity, of which we were speaking above — the subjectivity that is turned toward an object as a mere object. We shall soon see what sort of significance this factor has for the Biblical conception of truth. Love is the most active and personal thing we can think of. For this reason, the Bible always speaks of " hearty " love. In the love the whole person freely gives himself.

However, love is not only the most completely free, but at the same time the most completely dependent. While we are loving God — in the sense in which the Bible speaks of love for God — we know ourselves to be (as indeed we are) unconditionally dependent upon God, upon his giving love. Our creaturely love can be nothing other than the free return of that which God has first given us, of that which God in his love gives us — that is, himself, and therewith our actual life. We can give ourselves to God in love only because he has given himself to us. If already in the recognition of the Lordship of God our unconditional dependence upon God is known and acknowledged, this knowledge and acknowledgment is fulfilled in the love which is the answer to his freely given love — the love freely given without necessity. For this reason the Lordship of God — the dominion or Kingdom of God — first comes to fulfillment in this responding love.

God wills to be Lord; the *gloria Dei* shall be reflected in men: this is the dominion, the Kingdom of God. He can be Lord in the perfect sense only when he finds the fullest devotion given to him by those who have the fullest freedom, that is to say, in love. Similarly, it is true that his Lordship fulfills itself in his sovereign Creator freedom, that without necessity he gives being to his creature, so that in his giving the creature has life. The self-communication of God is the unconditional Lordship of God: even while God is communicating himself to the creature, he attains self-realization in the highest sense, his *gloria*. For this reason his self-affirmation fulfills itself in his self-giving, his glory as Lord in the choir of those who lovingly worship him as the inconceivably loving Lord. Thus God's will to Lordship — his holiness — points to his will to self-communication, his love in which his holiness is fulfilled; and his love points back to his will to Lordship as its presupposition.

But this is not to be understood as if in the final analysis Lordship or the holiness of God could be reduced to his love, so that it would suffice to speak about God's love. Not without reason the Bible time and again speaks of both as of two very different things. We cannot rightly understand the love of God — that is to say, understand it as freely giving love — if we do not understand it as the love of him who unconditionally wills to be Lord; nor can we rightly understand his Lordship in any ultimate sense if we do not understand it in relation to his loving will. Both exist necessarily alongside each other, yet not foreign to one another but one in reference to the other. In both, however, as Lord and as the boundlessly loving One, in his demand for obedience and in his self-communication, God is known as originally relating himself to a creature who is his counterpart, who in freedom returns what God has previously given him. It is thus with reference to the love of God (that love in which and

99

as which God has revealed himself to us) that we first understand in the full sense what it means that God is the God who approaches man and man is the man who comes from God.

5. Revelation and Knowledge of God

A further twofold factor can be understood at this point. Self-revelation and knowing, as we have said from the start, is always the decisive element in the God-man relation. Now we can understand why this is true: because God wills to be *known* as Lord. It does not satisfy him to be Lord over man as he is Lord over the subhuman creatures. He wills to be their Lord because only in his being *known* as Lord *is* he really Lord in the complete sense.

God is certainly also Lord over those who do not know him or obey him or love him — yet not in the full sense as when he is known as Lord. This is first really true in regard to fellowship. In some way God no doubt also has fellowship with the subhuman creatures whose life is derived from him without their knowing it. With them too he is, after all, the loving Giver, but not in the full sense.

He is loving Giver in the full sense less than ever when the human creature does not respond to his love. In this latter instance his fellowship with the creatures can reveal and realize itself only as his wrath, in that he holds them fast even in their rebellion against him. Yet in that relation he can never give himself in the true sense of his will to fellowship. Fellowship with God is present only when the creature meets his love with responding love, when the creature knows and appropriates his freely giving love.

Thus the knowledge, and the revelation in which the knowledge is rooted, is the decisive element as much in the Lordship as in the self-communication of God. Heat and motion can be communicated without revelation and knowledge, but not Lordship and the will to fellowship. The Lordship and love of God can be communicated in no other way than by his giving himself to be known and by his becoming known. Responding love

100

in essence means nothing else than that freely given love is recognized for what it is. In the final analysis existence *in* love and knowledge *of love* are the same.

Perhaps we should be more accurate to say (and this is the second point) that knowledge and act, knowing and *happening*, are in this instance a single process. God communicates himself *in* love: and this happens in the fullest sense only when his love is known in responding love. Unless this happening takes place, self-communication cannot consummate itself. It does not reach its goal. This act of divine self-communication thus brings together within itself the dual event of revelation and knowledge. In the responding love of the human creature the will of God is first realized: in the " yes " to the self-giving love of God, fellowship first takes its rise. The factor of knowledge thus belongs as the decisive factor to the act of self-communication.

All the formal concepts laid down earlier to characterize the divine-human relation have now been given their concrete content. Only in this way do they become intelligible in their essential interrelationship. This interrelationship is not a priori but of course entirely a posteriori, that is to say, grounded in God's act of self-communication. Since God's being as the Bible reveals it to us in no sense is being as such [An-sich-sein] but will to Lordship and will to fellowship, therefore it is essentially a related being — a being related to man, the creature who knows, acknowledges, obeys, and loves — a being related to the Kingdom of God. Because God is necessarily first and man second, the being of the creature, especially of the human creature, is receptive and rooted in the divine acting. Because God's will is both will to Lordship and will to fellowship, he wills to have a creature face-to-face with himself, who in freedom gives back to him what he first gives to the creature. Therefore, the act in which man receives the being to which God has determined him is an act of revelation and knowledge. Finally, this free face-to-face relation of God and the creature is essentially and necessarily grounded in the divine will to Lordship and fellowship. Consequently, it participates in the unconditioned character of the divine will.

God is thus the God who approaches man, and man is the man who comes from God, in order that God's will may fulfill itself in man's knowing and voluntary loving and that man's true life may be realized in his voluntarily acknowledging and affirming the divine acting and will. This two-sided but un-ambiguous relation, this state of the dependent-independent creature — to be face-to-face with God according to his will — is the fundamental category of the Bible; and in relation to it everything said in the Bible is said and must be understood. All that the Bible has to say about God's being and doing, about time and eternity, about the divine purpose and creation, about sin and redemption, about grace and works, about faith and repentance, about church and sacrament, is said within this basic structure and also formulates in a specific way this basic relation. Thus everything that theology avers must remain within this basic structure and everything that contradicts this funda-mental presupposition must be rejected and fought against as an unbiblical and even anti-Biblical error of speculation or doc-trinal distortion. We call this basic formal relation, which at the same time is identical with the contents of the whole Bible, *personal correspondence*. How the Biblical understanding of truth is determined by it we can already to some extent con-jecture. But it must be explained more completely and more exactly with respect to the epistemological problem of truth.

6. The Word and Faith

Two concepts that are constitutive for personal correspon-dence have not yet been specifically mentioned: that of the Word and that of faith. Of course, implicitly they were always pre-supposed. Revelation and knowledge belong in essence, as we saw, to the relation between God and man. God as Lord lays claim to the obedience of man; and by giving himself to be known as the loving God, he gives this love of his to man, that man may love him in return. He does both through his Word. For the Word is the way in which mind communicates with mind, subject with subject, will with will. The Word, on the

102

other hand, is that communication which does not convert the subject into an object; but when it is accepted it stimulates self-activity. The Word is the self-communication of God, which reserves an area of freedom for creaturely self-decision, which gives without violence, which so gives that the taking can be self-giving, voluntary self-giving.

The secret of the person is disclosed through the Word, in him who addresses as well as in him who is addressed. Only the Word is able to break through the infinite strangeness and the silent seclusion between persons: the Word unlocks person to person. But not the word of man: only the Word of God can accomplish this — why and how will be discussed later. In this place the only point to be made is that God's self-communication is made by the Word — a self-communication that at the same time reveals to man God's Lordship and love, in such a way that he acknowledges and accepts them. Since, therefore, the Word is the form and the means through which person reveals and gives himself to person, through which, therefore, fellowship between persons is created, it is through his Word that God realizes his will in and for man. Only the Word can put God's will before man in such a way that man's personality is acknowledged, that man can " react to it " in a personal manner, and answer it in decision. That God wills to have fellowship with man, to have man as an independent " other " who is yet wholly dependent on him, is manifest because God acts with man and upon man through the Word. Seen from the formal side, the Word is thus the center of the Biblical revelation as " the Son of Love " in whom God gives himself to man is the same center in material respect. Therefore, the Son is the Word and the Word, the Son.

What is analogous to the divine Word in man as the second member in the relation of personal correspondence? At first we might expect a concept such as that of hearing or perceiving as corresponding in man to the divine Word in God. This is, indeed, the case in the Old Testament. Since we are concerned with a correlative personal act, however, there should be more than a mere passive acceptance on the part of man. Mere

103

acceptance would be that mirrorlike subjectivity which can find place in relation to an object, but not between person and person. If what is said about personal correspondence as the fundamental category of the Biblical revelation is to be correct, a responsible act of man must correspond to the Word of God — an act in which the whole person is summoned and responds in order to receive the self-giving of God — a high, personal activity, the essence of which is this receiving. In the Bible, particularly in the New Testament, this act is called obedience-in-trust [*Vertrauensgehorsam*], *pistis*. The German word *Glaube*, connected in its original meaning with fidelity (loyalty) and love, has undergone such a shift in meaning that today it can hardly be used anymore for a translation of the New Testament *pistis*, unless through interpretation it is defended ever and again from the fatal intellectualistic misunderstanding into which it otherwise will necessarily fall.

Pistis, obedience-in-trust, is the personal answer of self-giving to the Word of God. In this response of self-giving, the divine self-communication first reaches its goal, and actual fellowship between God and man originates. In this two-sided yet unequivocal relation God is completely and wholly the Giver, the first, and man is completely and wholly the receiver, the second. In *pistis* is contained the personal acknowledgment of the Lord as Lord, obedience, and the personal acceptance of the divine self-giving love in grateful responding love. Faith is the complete self-giving of man which is consequent upon having received the unconditional self-giving of God. Faith is the single "answering" acceptance of the Word of God, the correct, fitting answer to the first freely given Creator-Word of God.

In the New Testament a rivalry (so to say) obtains between the two concepts *agapē* and *pistis* as the designation for this human behavior that corresponds to the divine behavior. Why was not simply *agapē*, the "love in the sense in which the Bible speaks of love," retained as the correct designation? While the Synoptic Gospels, and in a certain sense also the Johannine writings, in their connection with the Old Testament give the concept of *agapē* preeminence over the concept of *pistis*, Paul —

admittedly without any polemical purpose and also without simply displacing the concept of love to God — moved the concept of *pistis* into first place. The answer to the question of why he did this can be read only between the lines: the word *pistis*, obedience-in-trust, expresses more clearly than *agapē* the dependence of the human act upon a foregoing divine act. *Agapē* denotes *God's* act, the voluntary self-giving; *pistis* denotes, as something entirely and personally active, the receiving of this self-giving love, which admittedly as recipient of the divine love leads again to love. Paul thus wishes to say: Only on the ground of receiving the divine love, on the basis of *pistis*, can man love in the sense of *agapē*, and this, man's love, is then no other than divine love. It can be called *agapē* only insofar as it is actually divine love with which man loves God and his neighbor. Human *agapē* grows out of the *agapē* of God by virtue of *pistis*, by means of which man receives the divine *agapē*. It therefore becomes clear only in the concept of *pistis* that the correct human response is the answer to God's action toward man. What we have named the relation of personal correspondence thus first becomes fully clear in the correlation between Word of God and " faith." In this pair of concepts the Biblical understanding of the relation between God and man and therewith also the Biblical understanding of God and man finds its perfect expression. God is the God who approaches man because he wills to be known only in his Word; and man is the man who comes from God because only in " faith " has he his true being.

7. The Nature of Personal Correspondence Between God and Man

On the basis of what has just been worked out let us again consider the nature of this personal correspondence. Man trusts and believes the God who reveals himself in his Word as Lord and as Love. By this is not meant that man could also come together in this trust with another god or another person, as if the activity indicated in the word " faith " were a general possibility, which only this time becomes actual face-to-face with God, which another time might be realized with anyone. The meaning rather is: even as God the Lord is not " any " Lord but is *the* Lord, namely, the unconditional sovereign, the Creator-Lord; and even as God's love is not " any " love, but is *the* love, namely, the unconditional or voluntary self-giving love, so also " faith," *pistis*, is not " any " obedience-in-trust, but *the* unconditional trust and *the* unconditional obedience. Therefore, Paul can use *pistis* often in an absolute sense, without an object and without more precise qualification; he means " *pistis* simply," not any kind of *pistis* in a relative and otherwise used sense of the word.

This unconditional trust, this unconditional obedience-in-trust, is only possible where man meets unconditional sovereign power which at the same time is also unconditional love. To feel such trust toward every other person is not only not permitted but is not even possible: the phenomenologists would say " essentially impossible." *Pistis* in the New Testament sense is that total self-giving, that complete renunciation of one's own security, that utter dependence, which is only possible face-to-face with one whose being and acts are such that face-to-face with him one *can* afford to renounce his own security. Man stays concealed in his secure hiding place, secreted behind the walls of his I-castle; and nothing can really entice him out until one meets him who overcomes all the mistrust and anxiety about his very existence which drives him into self-security and there imprisons him. Man remains imprisoned within himself until the one meets him who can free him, who can break down his system of defenses, so that he can surrender himself, and in this surrender of self receive what he needs to enable him to abandon his securities; that is to say, until that one comes who gives man the life for which he was created. Only unconditional love, which brings man to self-fulfillment, and therewith gives him true selfhood and eternal life, can call out in him complete, unconditional trust.

The same holds for obedience, which together with trust forms a unity in " faith." Man can obey, in freedom, only Him who has an unconditional right to this obedience: the Creator-

Lord. But no command can compel this obedience, since enforced obedience is not real obedience. Real obedience is freely willed obedience: but this means an obedience fulfilled without the mental reservation, "How will I make out with this?" — hence an obedience that is given immediately with unconditional trust, in which he who obeys knows that he will not be a loser. For this reason only *the* Lord, who at the same time is voluntary, self-giving love, can find such obedience. As holiness and mercy are one in the nature of God, as the will of unconditional self-affirmation "over against" the creature and the will of unconditional self-giving to the creature are also one in His nature, so in "faith" obedience and trust are one, but only in that faith which does full justice to this God, and which by means of his self-revelation is called into being by him.

8. Faith as Dependence and Freedom

This "faith" — awakened through God's love — is also the only possible union of complete freedom and complete dependence. It is the most personal of the personal. In it the person is present wholly and without reserve; the "I" ventures to come out of its shell and in so doing takes over the entire responsibility for its acts. In contrast with this trust, everything else that man does is something partial, something that he cannot do "with the whole heart." For everything else that man does is conditioned: this alone is unconditioned. All else can satisfy only "one side of him": the whole man can only be satisfied when he himself becomes whole. Only in this way does he "come completely out of himself," with entire spontaneity, without stipulations and reservations. Only here is he entirely himself — "all there," so to say — for nothing else is big enough to enable him to achieve a complete personality, even though he may perhaps be striving to achieve it or affirm it. Consequently, only this faith is complete freedom.

On the other hand, only this faith is complete dependence. For it is release from the self, from what the self has, can do, or has done; release from glory in self and worry about self.

Faith means that man places himself completely in the hand of God: and even more, that he receives himself completely from the hand of God. In everything else that man does he holds himself back (so to say), he has a reserve, an if and but: he remains his own free lord. In this action man gives up his right of self-determination and places himself entirely in God's hand for disposal. Even more: he not only thus places himself for disposal, but knows and acknowledges himself as one who has been disposed of from eternity. This is the secret of election, which is faith's profundity. Of it something will be said later. Faith means that one lives his life as that which has been wholly given to him, and thereby knows that in this way he first is really himself.

If we now ask what has been the result of this inquiry into the understanding of truth with reference to gaining insight into the object-subject antithesis (determined by the rational, ordinary conception of truth), our answer can be only a preliminary hint, which will first be developed more exactly in the following chapter. If we ask what sort of truth man possesses in faith, what sort of truth he discerns in faith in God's self-revelation through his Word, it is as if with this question we had moved first of all into an entirely foreign context. In faith man possesses no truth except God's and his possession is not of the kind whereby one ordinarily possesses a truth, but personal fellowship. We are beginning to suspect why in the Bible the word " truth " appears in what is for us a strange context with the words " doing " and " becoming." Faith, which appropriates God's self-revelation in his Word, is an event, an act, and that a two-sided act — an act of God and an act of man. *An encounter takes place between God and man.* While God is coming to meet man he also makes possible man's going to meet him.

9. OVERCOMING THE OBJECT-SUBJECT ANTITHESIS

There is no longer a place here for the objective-subjective antithesis. The application of this pair of concepts in this con-

108

nection is entirely meaningless. The self-revelation of God is no object, but wholly the doing and self-giving of a subject — or, better expressed, a Person. A Person who is revealing himself, a Person who demands and offers Lordship and fellowship with himself, is the most radical antithesis to everything that could be called object or objective. Likewise, the personal act of trust is something quite other than subjectivity — that subjectivity which can become actual only when it is over against an object, that subjectivity which appropriates what is foreign to it. If we were to speak of appropriation in this context, it could be only of such a kind as when man gives himself to God to be owned by him. But if we know as believers, we recognize what is meant here, that that which happens in revelation and faith cannot be pushed into the framework of truth and knowledge of truth without its becoming in that way something quite different. Yet in the Bible what we have been talking about is just what is called truth. "I am the truth." This Biblical "truth" is as different from what otherwise is called truth as this personal encounter and the double-sided self-giving and its resulting fellowship are different from the comprehension of facts by means of reasoning. This is not to say that there do not also exist between both this Biblical and the general rational conception of truth positive relations outside of these differences; this question is to be discussed in the following chapters. Our first result is this: the concern of the Bible is personal correspondence as it is realized in the correlation between the Word of God and faith; and, contrariwise, such an understanding of the concept of the Word of God and faith as is yielded by reflection about the fundamental Biblical category of personal correspondence. Through it the Biblical conception of truth is determined and differentiated from every other understanding of truth.

10. The Origin of Man

In conclusion one further question might be answered, a question that in the course of our inquiry would necessarily arise without having gone into it any farther: of what kind of man have we been speaking thus far? Where is the man who answers God (as we have here supposed) while he obeys and trusts Him? Manifestly, we have not spoken here of actual man, otherwise our speaking would have had to be about sin. Hence, we have executed a thoroughly necessary abstraction. The concept of faith is more fundamental than the concept of sin; for sin is apostasy from faith, in which and to which man is called through creation. We need not presuppose sin to speak about faith; but we must presuppose faith to talk about sin. Not sin but faith is inherent in the created nature of man. In order to understand man and the man who comes from God we must be concerned, not with sin, but with faith. And we must, in order to understand what sin is, start our inquiry from man's " original position " from which he through sin has fallen and is continuously falling. In this connection the sentence holds: *verum est judex sui et falsi* — truth is judge of itself and of the false.

The actual man is the one whose existence is determined by this falling away from his original position, from his divine origin. How the problem of truth, as the Bible speaks of truth, is represented with regard to sinful man who is called to faith through Jesus Christ is the subject of the next chapter.

III

The Biblical Conception of Truth
and Faith in Justification

THE THESIS OF our first chapter was that the Biblical understanding of truth is of a different kind from the general
understanding of truth as determined by the object-subject antithesis. In the second chapter this thesis was clarified and
proved, in a preliminary way, through the development of the
fundamental Biblical category of personal correspondence,
which lies at the heart of the Biblical conception of truth. The
task of the present chapter is twofold: further to clarify and
prove this thesis by testing it with reference to a specified part
of the Biblical proclamation — faith in the justification of the
sinner; and to elucidate in such a way that not only it but also
this core of the Biblical message is thereby clarified. Since we
are concerned with a problem that on the one side is also the
subject of philosophy, a brief consideration of the relation between our inquiry and a philosophical inquiry is necessary.

1. THE OBJECT-SUBJECT ANTITHESIS IN THINKING

The antithesis or the correlation of object and subject has
dominated all Western philosophy since its very beginning.
Being and thinking, truth and knowledge — this is the problem
around which philosophical thought has turned at least since
the Sophists and Socrates — a problem that emerges again in
Kant's question about the relation between the " thing-in-itself "
and experience. The ultimate validity of this way of stating the
problem has not been questioned until very recently. One did

111

not ask if the truth could be found by means of these methods of reasoning, but merely which of the two great categories, the objective or the subjective, should be considered primary and what sort of relation obtained between the two. On this issue the great systematic trends of thought separated, realism with its primary emphasis upon the object, idealism with its primary emphasis upon the subject, pantheism or the doctrine of identity with its tendency to make the antithesis a matter of indifference. It was left for the newest form of philosophy, the existential, to question the validity of the antithesis itself. It is no accident that the source of this new thinking is to be found in the greatest Christian thinker of modern times, Søren Kierkegaard. It is therefore particularly suggestive for us theologians to attach ourselves to this philosophy, the entire bent of which seems to correspond with ours. Yet we must emphasize again that our considerations are purely theological, that hence they are not dependent upon the correctness or incorrectness of that philosophical undertaking which seems to run parallel — apparently or really — with our own. There are no preliminary philosophical judgments that we carry over to be added to theology; we are concerned rather with something *sui generis*, namely, the correlation between the Word of God and faith. The nature of this relation cannot be derived from any general philosophical propositions — were they even those of existential philosophy — but must be understood on the basis of primary knowledge of that correlation itself, as only faith can have such knowledge. It is only the *false* subordination of the correlation Word-of-God/faith under the object-subject antithesis and the concept of truth determined by the antithesis — hence, not what is essential but a *misunderstanding* — which compels us to use this general philosophical terminology.

At first it seems indeed to be a completely impossible undertaking to wish to withdraw oneself from between this pair of tongs (as it were) of the two concepts objective-subjective. They seem to be so necessarily linked with the process of thought as such that theological thinking too, it would seem, could not be done without them. As soon as one thinks at all, how can one help thinking "something," how help wanting to think what is objectively true? But we would thus concede that all thinking, including theological, takes place within this antithesis and is unable to proceed outside it. The theologian too when he thinks places the truth over against the false meaning; it therefore seems quite hopeless, even meaningless, to wish to attack this fundamental law of all thinking.

Indeed, for theology as the science of faith, as systematic reflection about faith in its relation to the Word of God, this law is valid. But the theologian is concerned, not with theology, but with the Word of God and faith. For the theologian this correlation Word-of-God/faith is the "theme" which he represents, which he portrays as "objectively" as possible — this must be understood first of all, although at once it must be more closely qualified and delimited. As thinker he succumbs, like every other thinker, to that fundamental relation of all thinking; he remains between the tongs (so to say) of the object-subject antithesis. But that *which* he is to comprehend is a "theme" *sui generis*; that with which he deals when he speaks about the Word of God and faith is precisely not thinking but a discerning of truth of an entirely singular nature. He should exhibit in its peculiarity what lies beyond the object-subject antithesis, the encounter between the self-revealing God and the man who, because of this revelation of God, surrenders himself. Hence, his "theme" — not his thinking about it — lies beyond what can be comprehended by means of the object-subject correlation. But not only this — and now follows the qualification and more precise delimitation of the concession granted at first: he cannot perceive this "theme" in a purely scientific way, but only if he himself becomes a believer: that is to say, only if he withdraws himself from the object-subject antithesis and meets in faith the God who meets him in the Word. This doubleness — that on the one hand he is a scientific thinker, comprehending objectively, and on the other, a believer — is the particular burden and difficulty of theology. The theologian is really a wanderer between two worlds.

2. Resolution in Faith
of the Object-Subject Antithesis

In thinking, the object-subject antithesis is present. But in faith, thinking is precisely what does not concern one. What is constitutive in thinking, that *I* think *something* — this distinguishing between the objective and subjective — finds no place in faith, if our understanding of faith (as it has been to this point) has the closest possible connection to the Pauline usage of the term. Of course there is also the colloquial way of speaking, "*I* believe *something*"; but at this point we give up the position we maintained when we spoke of the true Biblical faith; we give up the position of personal correspondence. In dealing with genuine, primary faith, i.e., when God reveals himself to me in his Word, we are not then concerned with a "something." In his Word, God does not deliver to me a course of lectures in dogmatic theology, he does not submit to me or interpret for me the content of a confession of faith, but he makes himself accessible to me. And likewise, in faith I do not think, but God leads me to think; he does not communicate "something" to me, but "himself." The counterpart is no longer as in thinking a something, a something pondered and discussed which *I* infer through the energy of my thinking, but a Person who himself speaks and discloses himself, who himself thus has the initiative and guidance and takes over the role (so to say) which in thinking I have myself. An exchange hence takes place here that is wholly without analogy in the sphere of thinking. The sole analogy is in the encounter between human beings, the meeting of person with person.

From this analogy are taken the conceptual means of expression with which we can represent in words what takes place between God and the man who has faith in the Word. Yet we are dealing *only* with an analogy seen in an exception to the usual occurrence, and we will speak about it immediately. The encounter between two human beings is ordinarily not personal at all but more or less impersonal. I see "someone." To see some*one* is not essentially different from seeing some*thing*. This someone says something to me. Someone saying "something" to me is not essentially different from my saying "something" to myself — that is, thinking. But now let us put the case that this someone does not say "something" but "says" himself, discloses himself to me, and that I, while he "says" himself to me, "hear himself"; and more, that while he discloses himself to me, and so surrenders himself to me, I disclose myself to him and receive him, while I surrender myself to him. In this moment he ceases to be for me a "someone-something" and becomes a "Thou." In that moment in which he becomes a "Thou" he ceases to be an object of my thinking and transforms the object-subject relation into a relation of personal correspondence: we have fellowship together.

Provided that this occurs in ordinary experience, the difference between the "something-someone," my object, and the "Thou," is, to be sure, relative, not absolute; the line of demarcation is not sharp — rather, the actual experience always has a mixed character. Consequently, this personal encounter and this fellowship are only analogous to what takes place between God and myself in the relation of revelation and faith. But this relative analogy can guide us even in what in faith is meant, not relatively, but unconditionally. We understand that when God speaks with me the relation to a "something" stops in an unconditional sense, not simply in a conditional sense as in an ordinary human encounter. When I stand opposite to God, I am face-to-face with him who unconditionally is no "something," who in the unconditional sense is pure "Thou." Therefore I have nothing to "think"; that is to say, I have nothing spontaneously to disclose. He alone is Discloser. In this relation of facing one another, not only that "which" is opposite becomes something other — a Thou instead of a something — but the entire relation undergoes a fundamental change, and that in the following way.

When I perceive "something," this "something" is then within me; it becomes, so to say, my possession. I embrace it.

In knowing it, I dispose of it. That which is perceived, that which is known, is at my disposal. The other side of this process is that I myself am not actually affected by it. My knowledge certainly enriches me; it may also have influence on my decisions, on my way of thinking; but it never penetrates to the core of my person — it does not transform "myself." *I* am, after all, the one embracing; I am the possessor.

A third point is to be noted. This knowledge unquestionably enriches me, it broadens my horizon; but it does not lead me out of my I-orbit, it leaves me solitary. This is also true if the object of my knowledge is human beings and if my knowledge about them is deeply searching: even then, since I know only about them, I remain solitary. Yes, even if these persons are not only known, but if they approach me, if they enter into relations with me, speak with me, if they in a relative sense thus encounter me and become "Thou" — even then I remain solitary until one of these persons does not merely say "something" and give "something" but discloses himself and so gives himself to me.

Knowing, thinking, possessing something, is thus, first of all, something over which I have disposal; secondly, something that does not essentially change me; and, thirdly, something that leaves me solitary. But if the Word of God meets me in faith, this is all reversed. Then I do not have something like property, which is at my disposal, but I myself become property; then I myself become disposable. This is what faith stammeringly says in the word, "My Lord." Faith says it, indeed, with the words denoting "having something," with the possessive pronoun "my" — for our speech is formed out of our everyday life, out of that life where we possess; and yet this "my" means exactly the opposite, not that God stands at my disposal, but I at his. Herewith, in the second place, a radical reversal occurs. Faith is no longer like that knowing which enriches, which leaves me unaltered in the core of my person; on the contrary, it precisely does not give me "something," but does change me in the very core of my person. Out of a lord faith converts me into a servant, and therefore

116

transforms the whole meaning of my existence. The "content" of my person, indeed, is left how and where it is, but the ruling principle is changed; much as if a man buys a house from another and does not alter the house but executes a "change of hands." That is faith: a change of hands, a revolution, an overthrow of government. A lord of self becomes one who obeys. And thirdly, solitariness is now also past. The imperious, reserved " I " is broken open; into my world, in which I was alone — alone too in spite of all my " something " and my " something-someone " — into the solitariness of the " Thou-less " I, God has stepped as Thou. He who believes is never solitary. Faith is the radical overcoming of the I-solitariness. The monologue of existence — even that existence in which many things have been talked about with many people — has become the dialogue of existence: now there is unconditional fellowship.

That God in his Word does not speak " something " but himself also changes the way of " speaking " God himself speaks to myself: that is to say, his speaking is address. Previously we expressed it in this way: God delivers to us no course of lectures in dogmatic theology; he submits and explains to us no confession of faith. He does say to me, " I am the Lord, thy God." His Word is claim and promise, gift and demand. Likewise " knowing " also acquires a new meaning. No longer is it a question of the insertion of something into the knowledge I possess, the expansion of the intellectual riches at my disposal; but it is answering personally when personally addressed, and hence obedient, thankful confession and prayer. Here, as above, the third person is replaced by the second person. " I am the Lord, thy God " bespeaks the answer, " Yes, I am thy obedient servant and thy child." The true form of faith is hence not the so-called declaration of faith, the formulated Credo that has been learned, but prayer, even as the Word of God is not a formula to be believed but challenging, freely given address. The antithesis between object and subject, between " something true " and " knowledge of this truth " has disappeared and has been replaced by the purely personal meet-

117

ing between the God who speaks and the man who answers. It is only *reflection* about faith that explains this personal occurrence in the second person as an impersonal twofold set of facts in the third person: a Belief signifying something to be believed, and belief signifying assent to this thing which is to be believed. Between the Word of God and the obedience of faith on the one hand and Belief-belief (Credo-credo) on the other lies an abyss, namely, the abyss that lies between the Biblical and the general, rational understanding of truth.

3. AGAPĒ

A short time ago we said that intercourse between human beings is an analogy — but no more — to what takes place between the Word of God and faith, with the exception of one instance where the analogy becomes identity. This instance in human relations which is not only analogy but the thing itself is called *agapē* in the Bible. The ordinary personal relation between persons is intermediate between the personal and the nonpersonal. In other words, the "natural man" knows the difference between person and thing, between "Thou" and "It," only in a relative sense. Of course conceptually we distinguish readily enough between an encounter with a person where the concern was only about "something" and an encounter where we met as "I" and "Thou," in which we disclosed ourselves to each other and so had fellowship together. And yet at the same time this "Thou" is for us always someone who is talked about in the third person, from whom we want something or whom we in some way would like to incorporate into our I-estate. What is lacking is the radical overcoming of the "I–It" relation by the "I–Thou" relation; what is missing is the radical relation of love. The "I" — as sinner, let us say now in anticipation — always confronts the "Thou" in a dominating and possessive relation that does not permit true fellowship to develop. The Bible tells us that in our own power we are quite unable to overcome the lack of fellowship between men, and that this can only be done where man

118

through God's Word receives fellowship with God through faith. When this faith actually comes into being, that change in the relation to men also takes place: the *agapē* of God becomes determinative also for the relationship among men. For "faith," *pistis*, is efficacious in "*agapē*"; only such a faith, says Paul, is meant and only such love is really *agapē*. But this does not happen when faith has the form of Credo-credo, that is to say, where the Thou-form of the occurrence has been translated into the It-form of reflection; it happens only when faith is a personal prayer in response to the personal Word of God. This faith proves itself at once and necessarily in *agapē*, while the other (as we theologians know particularly well) can be present very well with a complete want of *agapē*.

4. THE WORD OF GOD AND DOCTRINE

For the present we have aspired to nothing more than elaborating clearly the abysmal difference between personal faith, as we know it from the fundamental Biblical category of personal correspondence, and a Credo-credo faith that originates in the transition from the second to the third person, from the personal to the nonpersonal relation. Because of the entire church tradition and the Biblical usage of language, it is a matter of course that we must trace not only the antithesis but also the positive and necessary connection between these two very different conceptions of faith. For even if God does not deliver a course of lectures in dogmatic theology or submit a creed to us, but addresses us, so on the other hand it is not to be denied that in his Word God gives us himself in no other way than that he says "something" to us. In other words, even God's Word in some way contains doctrine, and even the faith that is the response of prayer contains knowledge. It will, therefore, be necessary to reflect more precisely about the relation between the personal and nonpersonal elements. The time has not yet come, however, for this reflection; we shall have to substantiate the knowledge just won before we can turn to the second task, or else we run the danger of losing all that has been gained. In which relation faith is to be considered — in the primary, personal sense or in the secondary nonpersonal, in the sense of second or in the sense of third person, in the sense of the response of prayer or in the sense of acknowledging a doctrine — is manifestly a very important and yet secondary question that we will take up in the next chapter. First of all, something else is necessary. Instead of speaking, as hitherto, about the Word of God and about faith in general terms, we wish now to approach the central point of the evangelical message, and test our previous statements with reference to that Word of God and that faith which are related concretely to our situation, that is, to the fact that we are sinners.

5. The Word of God in Our Sinful Actuality: The Law

The Word of God meets us in our actuality, as sinful men. It tells us that we are sinners, that we live in contradiction to our God-given appointment, that we have denied our dependence on God (in which we are created) through our misuse of the freedom of choice given us. In this way we have lost the fellowship with God that becomes actual only when we acknowledge our dependence on him. As sinners, we do not live without God, since God does not forsake us; but we live without fellowship with God, under his wrath. All of this is told us in the Scriptures, God's Word. Does, then, the Word of God after all tell me "something about myself"? Does it somehow describe a set of facts just like knowledge in the sphere of natural knowledge? Does it, then, reveal to us, as would a mirror held before the eyes, that which is in us, and tell us therefore what we could see in ourselves if only we could see accurately? Is this really the Word of God?

Indubitably it is, in a certain sense. The Word of God, provided that it does this, is what Paul terms "the law." We are judged according to the creation-established norm of our being, by the standard of what we should be according to the appointment of the Creator, and this judgment is as follows: We have missed our destiny, have perverted our being, and

120

therewith also have lost the life that was given us with our destiny. "Through the law comes knowledge of sin." Likewise, "The law worketh wrath." Both mean that the law reveals to us the opposition between the will of God and our being. The knowledge given us by the law does not disclose anything new about our being, but only makes apparent this being. With this set of facts the other as substantiated by Paul agrees, namely, that the knowledge of the law is a knowledge that man could attain by his own efforts, and that, to a certain extent, he does attain by his own efforts. The law is written in his heart, and the bad conscience is a sign of its efficacy.

For this reason the law is not the Word of God in the real sense. As Paul shows us in Galatians, it is preliminary and mediating; it has " come in between." God meets us in it, and yet he does not meet us as himself. Hence, no fellowship with God originates in the law; nothing new is created, but what is already in existence comes to be known. Paul says something even more daring about the law: it causes sin itself, although in substance it is divine. It is that kind of knowledge of God which is linked with our being sinners. The legalistic understanding of God's will makes us independent of God in a false way — in a way that corresponds to sin. It awakens the delusion in us — not by chance but necessarily — that we can do God's will by ourselves if only we want to; it seduces us to self-righteousness and self-glorification. In the light of the law we falsely understand — we sinners — God-given independence as independence from God; we think ourselves self-sufficient and self-existent. The legalistic understanding of God and our relation to him is therefore as false as sin itself; indeed legalism is actually the very heart of sin.

6. God's Act of Atonement Apart from the Law

When Paul begins to speak of the true Word of God after he has described the actual condition of man under the law, he inserts the words: "But now the righteousness of God, apart from the law, is revealed." He then discusses God's act of atone-

121

ment in Jesus Christ and the freely given righteousness of faith stemming from freely bestowed grace. Faith is not concerned with the law but only with the Word of God. With faith in this Word the legal relation between God and man comes to an end. In this Word man receives the new life; he becomes a new man. Of this Word alone it can be said that through it the love of God is poured out in our hearts and fellowship is established between God as Father and ourselves as his sons. We must hold to this conception of the Word of God if we would know what the Bible means by the Word of God in the real, strict sense.

God reveals himself, we explained earlier, in the justification of the sinner — reveals himself as Lord and unconditional love: that is to say, he reveals his unconditional will to Lordship and his unconditional will to fellowship. Paul draws both together into one concept which is hardly comprehensible to the Gentile: *the righteousness of God.* The meaning of the phrase can be discussed under three headings.

First, in this manifestation God reveals his essential being. He is the first, the One who is unconditional, freely ruling, bound by no presuppositions, the Creator-Lord. What he pronounces, happens; his Word is not derivative, but creative. If he says the prisoner is acquitted, then he is acquitted. This being of man, this new being which stands in contradiction to the old, has its ground and continuance only in his spoken Word.

Secondly, in this revelation God expresses his real being as love given without necessity, love given unconditionally. That the divine love is given without necessity is nowhere proved so unmistakably as when he gives his love to one who has forfeited it, who has merited his anger. God loves his enemies. But that is not all: he loves even those who wantonly utilize the highest gift he has bestowed on them — freedom — to turn against him. It thus becomes manifest that God's love is determined in no way by the worth or disposition of those loved, but absolutely by his willing to love them. His love is as freely given as it is unconditional. He gives it gratis, without any proviso except what is ineluctably part of giving, namely, that one accepts what is given. He gives love unconditionally to him who accepts it, which is to say, to him who believes.

Thirdly, while God is exercising his sovereign jurisdiction and his sovereign Creator-might, he is establishing at the same time unconditional fellowship. God is concerned about the revelation of his righteousness, about the manifestation of his majesty, his sovereignty; but while God expresses his Lordship, his unconditional sovereign honor — while he asserts himself as the Lord God — he gives himself to man at the same time in his Son, even while he takes on himself the whole threatening wrath, the whole curse of sin, and while he so manifests his will by giving everything to those to whom he has given himself in his Son. What does this mean in view of our question?

First of all, then, God in his Word of justification offers himself to men: that is, he offers fellowship with himself, and his very life. God does not merely say " something "; but while he says " something " he " says " himself, he manifests himself, he gives himself. A something no longer stands between God and man. This impersonal something was the law. Paul makes use here of the concept *gramma*, the letter. The task of the law is the task of the letter of the alphabet. The law is that which came between, an indirectness, an abstraction, something fixed, which undoubtedly indicates God's will, but in which God is not present as himself. The law is " a truth," something objective that one can know without in that way becoming essentially changed, an idea about God's will in which one has not to do with Him as One immediately present. That which has come between is removed; God has broken through the law as through the curse of sin, in his most personal Presence.

7. The Relation of Personal Correspondence in Sonship to God

Over against *gramma* Paul sets *pneuma*, the Spirit. God is present in his Word; his Word is Spirit and life. God does not will to exist as Something, as Abstraction, as an objective Given, as any Other; but rather as a personal, and therefore not a strange, Other, as One living within the hearts of believers, through the Holy Spirit testifying to himself as Father within themselves. An incomprehensible exchange now takes place. The human *I* is dethroned and God sets himself on the throne in man. The domineering *I* is "deposed" by the ruling Spirit of God. The Spirit of God bears witness to our spirit, that we are children of God. Yea, the Spirit itself cries, "Father." The Spirit of God himself prays in our prayers. The Spirit bears witness that the Father, who through the Son has come out of his mystery and drawn near to us, is *our* Father. He tells us that *we* are God's children. Consequently, it is God himself who does everything, upon which doing and saying alone man's new being depends.

And yet here, too, the relation of personal correspondence is not dissolved, but is first rightly established. It is God's righteousness, *sola gratia;* but it is at the same time the *righteousness of faith.* God speaks his Word and in his Word brings himself into the presence of man; but the real Presence actually comes first and only through faith, through that obedient trust and trusting obedience, that affirmation in which man surrenders himself to the God who has already given himself to man, in which man accepts God's Word of love. For this reason Paul speaks as often and as emphatically of a righteousness of faith as of the righteousness of God. We said that the love of God is unconditional: it makes only the condition which lies within its nature, that man accept it. God does not force faith upon anyone. None comes to faith except through the act of repentance and the act of trust. "Behold, I stand at the door and knock. *If any will open to me,* I will go in with him and sup with him." "*That whosoever believeth in him* shall not perish." "*To as many as received him,* to them gave he power to become sons of God, *who believed on his name.*" The Lord has given the invitation: but the question arises whether the ones who have been invited will come.

8. Personal Correspondence in the Obedience of Faith

As clearly and unmistakably as the Bible teaches God's all-efficiency in which everything is grounded, so it impresses unceasingly and indubitably that the Word of God *calls for* the obedience of repentance and faith. It is of the utmost importance to notice the particular passage in the letter to the Romans in which Paul first speaks of the Holy Spirit. It does not occur until the fifth chapter, after the discussion in the entire fourth chapter was about the obedience of faith. Through repentance and faith God imparts his Holy Spirit. Man, to whom the Word of Christ and the forgiveness of sins is preached, to whom God in his mercy offers himself, is not admonished to wait until the Holy Spirit is also given him — as if he himself could do nothing at all. Rather, he is told that he should believe the Word which is told him. The human subject, the human person, is not blotted out, is not ignored, but on the contrary is called up, is summoned in the most urgent way: Be reconciled to God! Hear, believe, obey, repent, and have faith in the Lord Jesus Christ!

This personal correspondence — this paradox for our thinking as determined by the object-subject antithesis — is set aside in no Biblical passage, but ever and ever again is emphatically stressed as the high point of the proclamation of grace. God wills to have a counterpart who in free decision says yes to him. God does not overwhelm man, he does not annul the human will, the power of personal decision, but makes a claim upon it. God is Lord; he is not causality. God does not make himself Lord in the manner of a superior force that overpowers what it meets, but he makes himself Lord precisely by means of this claim for faith and claim for obedience — and never otherwise. This point should be emphatically stressed because it is just in this area that time and again a non-Biblical thinking has transformed the idea of God into a doctrine about an abstract absolute. In this way the understanding of the Biblical message has been obscured.

Nowhere in the Bible is it stated that it is God who believes the divine Word, as the false objectivism attempts to maintain. In the Bible it is always man alone who believes, man alone who repents. But this faith of man, the affirmation of the Word of God, the acknowledgment of the Lordship of God in obedience, and the acceptance of the divine mercy in trust, is of such a nature that precisely in it man renounces his autocracy, thus relinquishing to the Spirit of God the throne of his I-lordship and giving up his place as lord of his life to God, the Lord. Beyond this the Bible never goes. For instance, it does not go in the direction of the doctrine of the sole-efficiency of God. The doctrine of the sole-efficiency of God has a Neoplatonic, not a Biblical, origin — even though it may have been defended by some of the most important teachers of the church. It is therefore not Biblical, because it sacrifices the fundamental structure of the Biblical proclamation, the relation of personal correspondence, to a way of thinking that is determined by the object-subject antithesis.

9. The Realization of the New Life

But in one other respect we must beware of a false objectivism. People have believed, supposedly in agreement with Luther but actually in contradiction to him, that one must understand the message of justification by faith alone in the sense of the later orthodox doctrine of forensic justification. This interpretation can in no way be blamed on Paul or, as has recently been shown, on Luther. The question involves the following: The Word of God promises us righteousness; it pronounces the sinner as righteous, which means as the one who is right with God, with whom God wills to have intercourse as with a son and no longer as with a rebel. This new status of the person — Paul calls it adoption into sonship — is grounded entirely in God's will and has its realization only in the Word of God. It is indeed as Luther said a " strange righteousness." " Christ is my righteousness." But the Bible, unlike many theologians, does not stop here. It goes farther and maintains that this righteousness actually becomes yours. God not only *declares*, he *creates* a new man. This new man is not only of a promised dimension, but one already realized if not yet perfected. So certainly as Christ, the living personal Word of God, does not *remain outside* ourselves but by faith *dwells* in us through the Holy Spirit, so certainly is the new man of no purely transcendent, eschatological dimension, but in faith is at the same time an experienced reality. We not only believe in the new man, but in faith we put him on, just as in repentance we not merely condemn the old man but actually put him off.

This realization of the new life is the content of the sixth chapter of the letter to the Romans. In faith the old man really dies; and in faith the new man actually lives. This is something quite different from maintaining that we merely believe that the old man is dead in Christ and that the new man lives in Christ. That is also true, but it is not the whole truth. Even while we believe that Christ died and rose for us, we actually participate in the dying and rising, and in this participation is our real new life. Thus here, too, personal correspondence is expressed in the Biblical proclamation. Christ *for us* corresponds to Christ *in* us; the righteousness *offered* us by God corresponds to the righteousness *accepted* in faith, which in being accepted comes to personal *actuality*. The new life is not only one in which we believe, but in faith it is real. Indeed, faith itself is this new reality. Man in faith *is* the new man, life in faith *is* the new life.

How could it be otherwise? God's Word is always creative. His promise too, since it is laid hold of in faith, is a new birth. Through the Word of promise we are born again to a new hope. To be able to hope, the certainty of hope, is already in itself a new personal life. A believing and a hoping person is a different person — if he really believes, if he persists in faith, if, as the Johannine writings always express it, he "abides in him." He who abides in God, in him God will also abide. Whoever abides not in God, in him God also will not abide. But whoever abides in him obeys his commandments and does his will. For the love of God is poured out in our hearts through the Holy Spirit. The "love of God in our hearts" is, according to Luther's word, *caritas*, with which the new man — in whom Christ through his Spirit is Master — meets God and his fellows. This love according to Biblical doctrine is not entirely in the future, but in believers is already of a realized dimension, even as the Holy Spirit, the pledge of the new life, is a present, creative reality in them.

Why is this so? Because in faith we are not dealing with a superior truth that remains over against us, but with the Word of God, by means of which God establishes fellowship with us. It is no accident that it was orthodoxy — to be sure very early in the age of the Reformation — which defended the doctrine of the purely forensic nature of justification. The significant factor in orthodoxy is that personal correspondence was crowded out by a conception of truth orientated about the object-subject antithesis. Orthodoxy thought of God as the teacher who delivered supernatural, revealed truth and proffered faith to man. In this way the Word of God was identified with doctrine, and faith was assent to this doctrine. Precisely that which is the concern of Biblical faith was consequently no longer understood: that is, overcoming the object-subject relation and having the real Person of God present in his Word, who as such is also the creative Presence of the Holy Spirit. For this reason the faith of orthodoxy was so destitute of love. For love cannot be created by faith in a revealed truth, but only by the presence in the heart of the Holy Spirit, who is none other than the very love of God himself poured out in our hearts. Faith in doctrine has never yet created new men: on the contrary, whenever it has usurped the place of true faith, which is fellowship with God, it has always been singularly lacking in love. This is not surprising in the light of what we have come to understand. Whenever the highest place — the place belonging by right only to living faith — is given up to faith in doctrine, an abstraction, a truth, receives the highest distinction; and the relation to persons must of necessity remain subordinate.

10. The New Relations with Fellowmen

In conclusion, these considerations lead us back once more to the connection between the divine and human Thou-relation, which earlier we wished to comprehend only as analogy. We have already spoken of the one instance in which it becomes more than an analogy. If it is indeed true that through faith we have real fellowship with God, that hence in faith the new person, the new man, comes to realization, then the new relation with fellowmen is also thus determined. The old relation was marked by the fact that in all social relationships there intruded that attitude of domination which the *I* assumes toward objects. The " Thou " was always at the same time someone, a subject for discussion, a third person, an object, and therewith at the same time " something " with which I start something, over which in some way I take command. But the change that takes place with faith will also change this relation. While man places himself under the Lordship of God, while man has fellowship with God who is love, his fellow is also face-to-face with him in a new way, no more as object but as " Thou." In faith we can regard our fellowman in no other way than that Christ meets us in him, Christ challenges us. The human lordly *I* is dethroned by the *I* of divine love; hence, faith is of such a nature that it proves itself efficacious in love. Through faith and through it alone our fellowman becomes, like God, an actual " Thou." For love, with which a man of faith meets his fellow, is after all not his, but " the love of Christ constraineth him." But while this love moves him, he has first become — or rather he has started to become — that for which he was created, a man who comes from God and goes to God.

IV

The Biblical Understanding
of Truth and Doctrine

THE PREVIOUS CHAPTER can be summed up as follows: The relation of personal correspondence, which we found to be the basic category of Biblical thinking and placed in contradistinction to the general understanding of truth, has conclusively proved itself to be at the center of Biblical faith in a primary and decisive examination of justification by faith alone. Faith does not depend on " something true " — even though this truth were something spoken by God — but has to do with God himself, as he reveals himself to us in his Word, is present with us, addresses us, and claims from us the response of obedience-in-trust. Conversely, our knowledge of the fundamental Biblical category has clarified the very nature of revelation and of faith, the justification of the sinner, in their true Biblical sense, and removed the encumbrances of the orthodox tradition. It will now be our task to develop this examination in relation to some more of the fundamental concepts of the Biblical message, showing how the basic category and content of the Bible — the formal and the material element — throw light upon each other.

1. THE POSITIVE RELATION BETWEEN THE WORD
OF GOD AND DOCTRINE

But first there is another problem to solve. Thus far we have elaborated only the negative relation between the Biblical and the general concept of truth, namely, the complete difference between the two. But we have already conceded, if only in passing, the one-sidedness of this interpretation. The relation between Word of God and doctrine cannot be fully stated by saying that they are " completely different." This is clearly indicated, not only by the whole history of the church, but also — and more significantly — by the content of the Bible itself. Even though it is true, as we previously said, that all doctrine in the Bible means nothing else and points to nothing else than that God himself addresses us in order that we ourselves may answer him in faith, it must surely be conceded at the same time that this address and this response can take place only by virtue of Biblical *doctrine*. Between the Word of God and obedience-in-trust on the one hand and doctrine and belief in doctrine on the other there must thus obtain necessarily and not only accidentally a positive relation in addition to the negative one. Of what sort is it?

Even as we previously said that the Word of God is not doctrine, that God in his Word does not speak " something true," but himself, so now we must further ask: Does he not speak himself to us in such a way that he tells us " something," " something true," so that doctrine after all is also contained in his Word? And if until now we said that faith, *pistis*, is something different from recognition of a truth, namely, trustful and obedient surrender to God, who imparts himself to us, so we must also further ask: Can this faith be consummated in any other way except that we believe " something " " which " God says to us? With this double query we neither shall nor may call in question what we have been pointing out: We continue to maintain that an abyss lies between what happens in the meeting between God and man in revelation and faith, what happens in this occurrence in the second person, and everything that has the form of discussion about " something true " in the third person. The question is whether this abyss is not bridged after all, whether in the act of God's speaking and man's thus being enabled in faith to hear and think, the positive relation between Word and doctrine is not already also established.

2. Jesus Christ Himself Is the Word

It is of the highest importance that Jesus Christ himself, the One in whom God imparts himself to us, is called " the Word." It is therefore he, this Person, who is really the Word. He himself is the communication, the self-communication of God; it is he himself in whom God proclaims and realizes his will to Lordship and his will to fellowship. The new point of view in the New Testament in contrast to the Old is that God proffers us his Word no longer only in the words of the prophets but in the Word become flesh. It thus becomes unmistakably clear that what God wills to give us cannot really be given in words, but only in manifestation: Jesus Christ, God himself *in persona* is the real gift. The Word of God in its ultimate meaning is thus precisely not " a word from God," but God in person, God himself speaking, himself present, Immanuel. " *I* am the Way, the Truth, and the Life." " *I* am the Light of the World." " *I* am the Bread of Life." " Come unto *me*, all ye . . . and *I* will give you rest." The incarnation of the Word, the entrance of God into the sphere of our life, the self-manifestation of God in his Son — this is the real revelation, the establishment of Lordship and creation of fellowship. Words, therefore, are not of ultimate consequence, not even divine words, but the Word, which he himself, Jesus Christ, is. Thus because he himself is the Word of God, all words have only an instrumental value. Neither the spoken words nor their conceptual content are the Word itself, but only its " frame," the means of conveying it. As God in his Word wills to direct not only our thinking but " ourselves," so in his Word he wills to give " himself " — that is, Jesus Christ.

3. Doctrine as Token and Framework, Indissolubly Connected with the Reality It Represents

But this is only one side of the matter. The other is that we cannot grasp this " content," the reality itself, except within this framework. The tokens are not accidental to but necessarily connected with the content; without doctrine the content is nonexistent for us. God indubitably says " something " to us in order to be present as Lord and as Father in the Son through the Spirit. Similarly, the direct address in its very simplest form — "I am the Lord, thy God" — when conceptually comprehended, conceals doctrine, "theology." God, to be sure, does not deliver to us a course of lectures in dogmatic theology or submit a confession of faith to us, but he *instructs* us authentically about himself. He tells us authentically who he is and what he wills for us and from us. And similarly, even the simplest and most direct, the most immediately personal, response of prayer, has its conceptual content: "Our Father who art in heaven." Consequently, we can never separate the abstract framework from the personal Presence contained in it, although certainly we must differentiate them. We know that we can never have the one without the other, and we know at the same time that the whole point is to have the personal contained within the abstract framework. Doctrine is certainly related instrumentally to the Word of God as token and framework, serving in relation to the reality — actual personal fellowship with God; but doctrine is indissolubly connected with the reality it represents.

In this connection we may remind ourselves of the sacraments. As God himself is present with us in the bread and wine of the Lord's Supper, in these tokens, so the Word of God wills to be present with us in words. This elucidating reference to the Sacrament is instructive in two ways. On the one hand, the Sacrament as the *verbum visibile* teaches us that the reality itself is not identical with the words, nor by any means fully represented in them. Especially while taking part in the Sacrament, we see and are given the signified reality, and thus are freed from an idolatry of words; our Lord instituted it precisely to show us that what is of moment is he himself, not doctrine about him. In order to be present with us he himself can utilize in a sovereign way this *verbum visibile*, which is not exactly language in the ordinary meaning of the word. On the other hand, it becomes clear in the Sacrament that the token is indissolubly connected with the reality signified. Our Lord wills to be present with us, not "behind" or "beside" but "in, with, and under" the token of the Sacrament. The idolatry of the token is error on the side of magic, the "cursed idolatry," as it is called

133

in the Heidelberg Catechism; the separation of token from the reality signified is the error of the "sacramentarians," against which Luther rightly fought. What is of moment is that our Lord himself is present; but he is present only "in, with, and under" the token, be it doctrine or Sacrament to which we refer.

4. The Limited Yet Indispensable Nature of the Concept of Truth Determined by the Object-Subject Antithesis

The question with respect to our central problem is: The concept of truth determined by the object-subject antithesis which deals with "something true" is indeed foreign to what is ultimately the concern of faith. The fact remains that in faith we are dealing, not with truths, not even with divinely revealed truths, but with God, with Jesus Christ, with the Holy Spirit. But, on the other hand, this conception of truth or the truth presumed in it is indispensable as instrument, as framework, as token of that which is the concern of faith. Faith, in other words, is in the final analysis not faith in something — something true, a doctrine; it is not "thinking something," but personal encounter, trust, obedience, and love; but this personal happening is indissolubly linked with conceptual content, with truth in the general sense of the word, truth as doctrine, knowledge as perception of facts. God gives himself to us in no other way than that he says something to us, namely, the truth about himself; and we cannot enter into fellowship with him, we cannot give ourselves to him in trustful obedience, otherwise than by believing "what" he says to us. Since, therefore, this conjunction of token and reality, of signification and what is signified, is already given in the act of divine revelation, we call the connection not only instrumental but sacramental.

5. The Connection Between the Two Concepts of Truth

The connection between the two conceptions of truth has not yet been sufficiently clarified to avoid the possibility of deviating toward a false objectivism or an equally false subjectivism. In agreement with the whole church we say that the Bible, Holy Scripture in its entirety, is the Word of God. As in its totality it is event, so in its totality it is witness. But to this first assertion a second must at once be added. Not everything in the Scripture stands in the same connection to the essential meaning. As I have pointed out elsewhere with reference to the church, so in the Bible it is true that there are differences between what is contiguously and what is more distantly connected to this essential meaning; there is *a connection more intimate or less intimate.* Carefully to note this difference is a matter of the highest importance; not to do so is a serious subversion to faith and the church. There is nothing in the Bible that is not connected with what is its central concern; for everything after all is linked with the sequence of events in the history of revelation, with the truth content in the revelation of the living God who has conclusively made his name known to us in Jesus Christ. But it is foolish to maintain that everything in the Bible — for example, detached bits of historical narrative — is connected in the same way to its essential content, to Jesus Christ, to the Word of God. There are, for example, the local references in the Gospels, which indeed are not inconsequential for a knowledge of Christ, for it is of the greatest importance that Jesus Christ lived and suffered, not just anywhere, but in specific places. And yet the local references considered singly are for the most part not of great importance, and not too much depends upon whether or not they are right. Similarly, Jesus Christ is not revealed to us otherwise than in the history of Jesus of Nazareth; but most of the single items of this history are not of the same decisive importance as the fact of his death on the cross. Likewise, much in the letters of the apostle Paul is indeed not inconsequential for an understanding of his message; and yet it would be absurd to maintain that the list of greetings in Rom., ch. 16, is as momentous — is the Word of God in the same sense — as for instance vs. 21–31 in the third chapter of the letter to the Romans. The Bible, figuratively speaking, is not a level plain, but a crater in which everything is orientated about one point. The nearer one is to this point, the nearer he is to what is quintessential. The Reformers suggested a similar difference when they separated the " history " from the " doctrine " — as, for instance, Luther did with reference to the Christmas "history." The primary concern, he said, is not so much with the " history " — by which he meant the self-evident, detached items — as with the " doctrine " — by which he meant the actual occurrence of salvation and revelation, the Word becoming flesh. In " doctrine " God tells us who he is and what he wants with us; hence, through it we have fellowship with him. Of course, this does not destroy the force of what was said at the beginning of the second chapter about history and doctrine, namely, that narrative and not doctrine is the adequate form to express the essential message of the Bible. This message is that " narrative " which is caught in one sentence in the Fourth Gospel: " The Word became flesh, and we beheld his glory." Insofar as the " doctrine " in this Johannine word depicts this happening, it is immediately close to what is central, to what is essential, in the Bible.

Similarly, the church in every age — although not always with the same energy and the same expert knowledge — differentiated between the chief article of faith and other doctrines that also necessarily belong to faith, but in whose case the tendency to error was less dangerous than with the cardinal doctrines. It is not without danger to make such distinctions, but the danger is even greater if one does not make them. For then every believer would actually have to be a learned theologian in order to be saved. In every correct catechism such a selection is made on the basis of more or less understanding of what is central. Perhaps one would need to say that this selection could not be the same for every age, since the question is not one of working out a timeless system of " central truths of faith," but of fighting a war in which the areas of combat (so to say) are especially appointed for every age. The discussion of this question, however, would carry us too far afield. In any event it must be clear on what basis the selection is made and why it is legitimate: it has to do with the closeness of connection to God's immediate address in Jesus Christ himself. The more unmistakably a doctrine

136

points to this connection, the more the "something" which is said constrains the thoughts to turn from looking at "something" to looking at "himself": the more, therefore, the testimony about God enables one to hear his address, so much more immediate is the something, the doctrine, connected with the primary concern of the Holy Scriptures.

6. GOD'S FREEDOM IN HIS REVELATION

But this principle of contiguity, which is also the means of distinguishing between pure and corrupt doctrine, must be narrowed down at once to its specific value by means of its opposite: God can speak to us by means of a word whose contiguity to what is essential could not be known by itself without taking into account that particular event of divine speaking. "The Spirit bloweth where it listeth." God, because he willed it so, has indeed bound himself of his own free will, by means of his historical revelation, to this happening which we call the history of revelation and salvation, the witness of which we have in the Holy Scriptures. Even as he spoke, as the living God, with Moses and Isaiah, not with Buddha and Lao-tze, so he gives us his Word in the Bible and not in any other religious book of the East. At all events he binds us unconditionally to this book, because he binds us to this history. But it is his free will and his gift, whenever and wherever through the Holy Spirit he actually wills to reveal his revelatory Word, wherever and whenever through the Word of Scripture he himself wills to speak to us. To be sure, it can happen that the whole Bible remains closed to a man until all at once the meaning of one word strikes him — a word that by all theological criteria we should least have expected to have such evocative power. Indeed, we must go farther and say: God can, if he so wills, speak his Word to a man even through false doctrine and correspondingly find in a false Credo-credo the right echo of his Word. This is no license for careless teaching and preaching or for theological relativism; for *we* are restricted to his historical revelation as well as to the witness to it and therewith also to the principle of contiguity

137

and the separation indicated by it between pure and corrupt doctrine. But God is not thus restricted, and his freedom limits the validity of that principle of contiguity and in the last analysis of pure doctrine. Even the closest connection of doctrine to the Word itself, as it occurs perhaps in central utterances in the New Testament, therefore remains incommensurable with God's own Word, in a free relation, ultimately determined only by God's will, even though for us this freedom does not exist.

A concluding word must be said about the relation between God's Word and doctrine, and here we will use to good advantage for our formal problem the knowledge gained in the preceding chapter about the antithesis between law and gospel. Doctrine seen by itself, that is, separated from the Word of God as the event of encounter, stands in the closest relation to the law. The possibility certainly exists that in his faith a man stops dead with the law as such and does not attain personal, spirit-produced and spirit-filled obedience-in-trust. Not only " can " this occur; rather this is the great negative experience of the church in all centuries. Insofar as this happens, doctrine — perhaps the doctrine laid down in the confession of the church or in dogma or in the catechism — is for man nothing other than law. In his faith he is not dealing with God himself but with something true about God, with true doctrine about God. He has been challenged in the name of God — under appeal to the authority of God and that of Holy Scripture — to acknowledge something as true, without God himself through the power of the Holy Spirit transforming this " something true " into personal fellowship with himself, without the man surrendering himself to God in trustful obedience. The challenge to believe — " you must believe that as God's Word " — remains for him in that foreign and impersonal area in which the law is, as long as it is only law; and correspondingly his obedience in meeting this claim is obedience as a meritorious achievement, which is the only possible way to confront the law.

Whatever the content of this doctrine may be — it may be even the doctrine of atonement through Jesus Christ and of justifying faith — so long as it is not God himself who speaks

138

with man and while speaking meets him in fellowship, so long as doctrine confronts him as something taught by church or Bible "which one must believe if he wants to be a Christian," his relation to it remains legal and bears all the marks of legalism. Even Jesus and the grace of God is then law — *gramma*, the letter. But that has not happened upon which everything — everything! — in true faith depends: that through the Holy Spirit Christ himself dwells in him. The love of God has not been poured out in his heart through the Holy Spirit. He believes in the Holy Spirit — because the Scripture speaks about him — but he has not received the Holy Spirit, the Holy Spirit has not taken up dwelling in him; the Holy Spirit does not motivate him like the children of God, does not guide him, does not make him joyous, does not make him free. He who believes solely in doctrine only knows that these are all activities of the Holy Spirit — that is, after all, what the Bible teaches — but these activities do not occur in him; for this "letter" too, as well as every other, has no living strength.

This faith, as the Reformers repeatedly point out, is therefore dead, powerless, and wholly without worth. It is a deception, a facsimile of the true faith, a counterfeit bill that has exactly the same markings as a good one, but the signature, the certification, is lacking. This faith is not written in the heart by the hand of God, but only by the hand of the church, by the hand of the apostles. The confusion of real faith with this faith, which clings to dogma or to literalism in Biblical interpretation, which confuses mere doctrine, even though it be Biblical doctrine, and the formulated Confession, the "something true," with the living Word of God, is a tragic blight that lies over the whole history of the church. It is no accident but a necessity, as we now know, that this faith in dogma takes its rise in the church at the same time with moralistic legalism. This "Credo-credo faith" very early — manifestly already at the time when The Letter of James was written as warning against it — usurped the place of genuine faith, paralyzed the church, and perverted its will.

But as the law, even though it is done away with in Christ,

is a tutor to bring us unto Christ, a divine "stronghold" (*phroura*), which "directed men to Christ," so also is this faith in dogma, this legalistic Bible-faith. Since God does not speak with us otherwise than as he "says something" to us in order to communicate himself, so a certain amount of doctrine must be present before living faith can come into being. Of course this can be an extraordinarily small amount. That jailer was changed in one night from a pagan into a believer. This conversion manifestly took place with a minimum of doctrine; the same obtained with those "three thousand souls" who on Pentecost "were added." If he has once become the teacher, God requires few words in order to teach; and because he is the teacher, it requires under certain circumstances a very small measure of doctrine on the part of man. The relation between doctrine and Word of God, we said, is in the last analysis incommensurable. It must suffice to recognize that an abysmal difference, and yet at the same time a necessary connection, lies between the two. Doctrine alone without the presence of the Holy Spirit is law and betokens legalism; but human boasting about the freedom of the spirit without doctrine is egoistic enthusiasm. The Reformation insight remains valid: Word of Scripture and Word of Spirit, personal directness in doctrinal indirectness, even as Jesus Christ must fulfill the law in order to free us from it.

7. The Doctrine of the Triune God

Only now are we in a position to undertake an examination and clarification of our thesis with reference to the primary content of the Biblical message; for we know now what each separate doctrine means: Each points to God himself in his will to Lordship and fellowship, and to God himself in his act which creates this Lordship and this fellowship.

The doctrine of the Triune God expresses just such a content. To be sure, at first it might seem as if this doctrine were an instance contrary to our tenet, that the God of the Bible is always the God who approaches man, whereas the content of this doctrine is God as he is in himself, whose nature it is to be self-sufficient, who being from everlasting to everlasting has created the world in time not because he had to but because he willed to, who hence cannot be thought to be (like the " Godhead " of pantheism) only in everlasting correlation with the world and man. Is this not precisely the meaning of the doctrine of the Trinity, that God, independent of the being of the creature, is in himself the loving One, the self-communicating One, the One who speaks? Certainly this is the content: God, who in himself is Father, Son, and Spirit, who hence did not first need the world and man in order to be Father, Son, and Spirit. But the relation of this perception to our thesis is, not of a contradictory, but of a corroborative nature.

For this is just the meaning of the mysterious doctrine of the Tripersonal God: God as he is by and in himself, in his unfathomable mystery, is none other than he who has manifested himself in his revelation in Jesus Christ as the Lord and as the loving Father. The doctrine of the Trinity, the doctrine of the everlasting love of the Father for the Son and of the Son for the Father through the Holy Spirit, attacks the notion that God as he is " by himself " is another than God as he is " for us " in his revelation. " If you ask who he is: He is called Jesus Christ, Lord God of Sabaoth and is no other God." God is therefore through all eternity the loving One; he is in himself the loving One; the being of the creature, which indeed is realized in time in the act of creation, is established through all eternity in his loving purpose, in the loving nature of God. He has loved us through all eternity and elected us in his Son who is love, who therefore is named the firstborn before all creatures. God wills — even when we think about him as he is in himself — to be known as no other than that One who meets us in Jesus Christ, his Son, as the God who approaches man, the God who would communicate himself and who in his self-communication glorifies himself. We should not speculate about a " God-in-himself " [" Gott-an-sich "] as if he were some other than the God who reveals himself in Jesus Christ as the loving Lord; but we should know that through all eternity he is this One and no

141

other, the Father, the loving One who imparts himself.

Consequently, the doctrine of the Trinity, as Luther and Calvin stressed time and again, is more a delimiting and safeguarding doctrine than a Biblical kerygma. The Bible does not guide us to reflect about God as he is in himself — the doctrine of the Trinity time and again misled theologians into unprofitable speculations; but it guides us to recognize the Father in the Son through all eternity. It diverts us from unprofitable speculation about God as he is in himself through reference to God's historical revelation, to the God who meets us in his Word and in his act, and declares only this about God as he is in himself, that he is no other than the Being disclosed to us in the historical revelation.

8. THE DOCTRINE OF ELECTION

Just as little do the Scriptures teach us about a secret *double decree* of God. Whenever they speak of the eternal decree of God, they proclaim the decree of election and nothing else. The doctrine of the double decree is not Scriptural, but a speculative enlargement of what is given in the Scriptures. Even the ninth chapter of the letter to the Romans, which so often is cited as the *locus classicus* of the doctrine of the double decree — that some are predestined through all eternity to everlasting life, others through all eternity to everlasting damnation — says nothing about it, but teaches the complete sovereignty and freedom of the divine compassion. God's compassionate love for us has no other ground than his free, unnecessitated love. The creature has no claims upon God, God owes him nothing — he after all is the creature's Lord. That he has compassion for him is due to his love given without necessity. This eternal election is the holy secret of faith. This is what God says to him whom he creates his child in Jesus Christ and to whom he therefore promises eternal life, while through this his Word of love calls faith into being in him. Consequently, the eternal decree of God should always be spoken of only in correlation with faith. Those elected are the same as those who love God. Election and faith, election and love of God, are correlative concepts in the Bible. To be elected and to be one in whom the love of God is poured out through the Holy Spirit is one and the same thing. All speculations about election outside of this correlation — this personal correspondence — should be avoided, as the preacher Luther always stressed. We should not grant leeway to the desire for intellectual investigation for its own sake, which is all the time spinning out more and more detailed questions; and the raising of impertinent questions should be discontinued. You wish to know who God is and what he wills? Then cling to his revelation in Jesus Christ; then believe in him. Do this and you will know yourself to be elected; do not do it and you are lost. But then there is also nothing more to say about the eternal decree of God, for God's Word speaks of that decree only as it is known in faith.

This incongruity and incompleteness, so annoying to this desire for intellectual investigation for its own sake, is the distinguishing mark of all Biblical doctrine over the question. For this reason the Biblical doctrine of election is a pattern for what we have shown to be the basic structure of Biblical thinking in the concept of personal correspondence. The thought of the double predestination originates in overstepping the delimitations of this doctrine drawn in the Bible. It originates, considered essentially, in the non-Biblical thought of the sole-efficiency of God or of the absolute God. It is therefore a temptation that lies very close to everyone who once knows about election — a temptation that we should withstand. The thought of the eternal decree in the Bible is the same as the thought of the eternal consummation in the Kingdom of God. The Bible has nothing to say about a *gloria Dei* that fulfills itself in the misery of the damned. For the *gloria Dei*, as we shall later show, is identical with the consummate praise of God by the creature.

The logically unsatisfying nature of this doctrine — in distinction from the system of complete logical equipoise in the doctrine of the double decree — is always the sign that the relation between God's grace and man's decision can never be logically determined. We have only the two possibilities: either the logically satisfying system of equipoise, satisfying the claims of thought, whereby either divine sovereignty or human freedom, and hence the reality of decision, is nullified; or the validating of both the divine sovereignty and the reality of the free decision, whereby the logically unsatisfying paradox takes its rise. The doctrine of the double predestination is not paradoxical — it is logically satisfying — but it sacrifices the reality of human decision to determinism; that is, it evades the basic Biblical structure of personal correspondence, which from its point of view is a logical annoyance. That subsequently, after this logical system of equipoise has transformed the freedom of decision into a mere appearance, the claim is made that human freedom is nevertheless still a reality, by no means makes the system, as such, paradoxical. It merely means the affirmation of something that by definition is ruled out. The claim of freedom comes too late; the system is closed, there is no place for it. The logical conclusion ruled it out. Theological thinking has here become metaphysical. The Biblical idea of God, in the last analysis, is crowded out by the philosophical, speculative one. The system of truth has become master over the Biblical faith in the God who always, while summoning to faith, demands decision. It is therefore important to note that a theologian like Calvin, because he is essentially proclaimer of the Biblical word and not essentially thinker, never preached the doctrine of the double predestination but only expounded it in theological polemical contexts. Surely he suspected that this doctrine is not the concern of the Biblical message but the product of speculative thinking.

As the Bible thus speaks of the eternal divine decree — namely, the decree of election — the close connection between God's will to Lordship and will to fellowship on the one hand and man's complete responsibility on the other becomes fully apparent. Man's responsibility is grounded precisely in his having been elected. It is precisely out of the Biblical doctrine of election that the Biblical ethic develops. To the divine election there corresponds on man's side the obedience of faith and love.

144

Indeed, one may put the Biblical view even more sharply: Man's election of God as the Lord corresponds to God's election of man. One passage in First Corinthians illustrates this point. In the eighth chapter, where Paul speaks of knowledge, we read: " Knowledge puffeth up, but love edifieth. If any man thinketh that he knoweth anything, he knoweth not yet as he ought to know; but if any man loveth God, the same is known by him." Being known by God is the same as being elected, and being elected corresponds, like the divine love, to man's love for God. Likewise, we read in the *locus classicus* of the New Testament doctrine of election, Eph. 1:4: " He chose us in him — in Christ — before the foundation of the world, that we should be holy and without blemish before him in love." I know of no more complete expression of what I mean by the fundamental Biblical relation of personal correspondence than in these two passages.

9. THE IMAGO DEI

From the *doctrine of creation,* which we placed at the beginning of all our considerations, I should like in this connection to examine only the Biblical thought about the *creation of man in the likeness of God.* What our thesis expresses is actually applied at this point to the theme of Biblical doctrine. What is meant by the idea of the *imago Dei* in the Holy Scriptures?

At all odds this is clear first of all: In man, God created something special, one excellent creature above all others, whose distinctive feature is that in some sense he is similar to the Creator. To me it is quite probable that the Old Testament passages which deal with the image of God in man at first wanted to say nothing else than this: Man is different from other earthly creatures because of the divine likeness given him by God, the most apparent expression of which is his power to rule over the other creatures. Man is derivative person, even as God is original Person. But even when we are thinking in terms of the Old Testament we may not lift this idea out of the entire context of the Biblical revelation. That man is derivatively what God is orig-

145

inally is for believers in the Old Testament most important of all in this connection. God's relation to men is different from that which he has to other creatures. The superior position of man in the hierarchical order of creatures as such, however, is not important just here. He has intercourse with man; he reveals his will to him and expects obedience and trust from him. It is not that man as he is in himself bears God's likeness, but, rather, that man is designated for and called to a particular *relation* with God.

In the Old Testament what we have called the relation of personal correspondence stands out (if I may so express it) in bold relief. Certainly, God is always first, the Creator, the Giver from whom man has received everything that he has and is. It is, after all, God who has created him in his own image, who has given him his especially distinctive being and appointment. God's covenant with the people of Israel is similarly a covenant of grace, as the covenant with Noah was already a covenant of grace, originating in God's mercy and sustained in unutterable patience despite all the unfaithfulness of man. But man's being a free person, face-to-face with God, is stressed in the Old Testament with extreme urgency. " See, I have set before thee this day life and good, and death and evil. In that I command thee this day to love the Lord thy God, to walk in his ways, and to keep his commandments, that thou mayest live. . . . But if thine heart turn away so that thou wilt not hear, . . . I denounce unto you this day, that ye shall surely perish. . . . I have set before you life and death, blessing and cursing: therefore choose life, . . . that thou mayest love the Lord thy God, and that thou mayest obey his voice, and that thou mayest cleave unto him: for he is thy life." (Deut. 30:15 seq.)

The grace of God is first; yet it is not forced on man, but submitted to him. He is not overwhelmed by it, but he is treated as one who can and should make free decisions. Grace must be accepted by man: The love of God, if it is actually to come to life for man, must be responded to with answering love; God's Word of compassion, the freely given Good, if it is really to become a blessing, must be heard and retained by man. God binds

146

himself to man while making man's salvation the concern of his almighty will; but this binding requires the human response of man's binding himself to God. This is the divine conditional, the divine-human *if*, the fixed fundamental law of the God-man relation in the Old Testament. Undoubtedly man is sinner, he is unfaithful, he denies; but God is compassionate and forgives sin. However, this covenant is conditional, as Ps. 103 shows us: He is "compassionate to those who sustain his covenant and remember his commandments, to do them." God wills to have as his counterpart a person with the power of free decision who in love responds to His love. This is the connection in which the concept of man's being made in the image of God is to be understood.

Herewith a connection is also made with the use of this concept in the New Testament. There the concept of the *imago Dei* undergoes a radical transformation. There are, indeed, passages where the exact likeness of God is spoken of in the Old Testament sense as the essential characteristic of man as such, of everyone who bears the human face. (Luther no doubt noted this double usage of language and differentiated between the one as the *similitudo publica* and the other as the *similitudo privata*.) But in the critical passages that deal with the exact likeness, the presupposition is that man has lost this divine image and that it must be and will be restored through Jesus Christ. The connection with the innate image of God is not, however, given up. The New Testament does not further explain how both have a relation to each other — that every man is created in the exact likeness of God, and yet that as sinner he has lost that image so that only through Jesus Christ it can be restored again. To arrive at an explanation of what happens between the impressing of the divine image and its being lost, we must make use of a process of "extrapolation" (so to say). To say that man has lost the image of God indicates that one no longer means by this expression the same thing as the Old Testament meant by it: being person in the sense that every man, whether sinner or not, whether believer or not, is person as differentiated from the subhuman creature; for *this* essence

147

of being a person is certainly not lost. The New Testament, rather, means more precisely what we have won again, by the grace of God in Jesus Christ, fellowship with God, essential humanness. To *this* image we are restored through Christ.

With the *imago Dei* concept a further transformation has taken place: From a concept expressing a static characteristic it has become a concept of relation. " But we all, with unveiled face, beholding as in a mirror the glory of the Lord, are transformed into the same image from glory to glory." (II Cor. 3:18.) Paul depicts here the relation between man and Christ as that between a source of light and a mirror, but with the modification that the mirror through the additional influence of the source of light gradually becomes an all-powerful reflector. The *imago Dei* is no longer a human characteristic that God once for all impressed upon man at the time of his creation; rather, it is now something that originates in Christ and man actually being face-to-face, in the influence of His " countenance," He as archetype forming the man who in faith appropriates that influence.

In this way we can state — one might almost say with conceptual theological precision — what we mean by the relation of personal correspondence. God creates for himself in Jesus Christ through the Spirit a personal counterpart, who gives back to him in a personal act what he has first received, love and the praise of God's glory. Man first becomes — after as sinner he had ceased to be so — similar to God by means of the love of God given to him in Jesus Christ, poured out in his heart by the Holy Spirit, which now also shines out from him in a manner commensurable with the Word of faith that proves itself efficacious in love, and in fulfillment of the words: " Let your light so shine before men, that they may see your good works and glorify your Father who is in heaven." We also think of the word in the letter to the Philippians: " That ye may become blameless and harmless, children of God without blemish in the midst of a crooked and perverse generation, among whom *ye are seen as lights* in the world, *holding forth* the word of life " (Phil. 2:15).

148

This Pauline *imago* concept embraces in a remarkable way the anticipatory grace of God, Source of all life and good, the effectualness of this grace through the Word of God, the personal presence of God in Jesus Christ, the pure receptivity of the man in faith, and the free return of what has been received in reciprocal love. In two other important passages this new concept of the *imago Dei* is brought into clearer connection with man's freedom or his power to make decisions. " Put on the new man, that after God hath been created in righteousness and holiness of truth." (Eph. 4:24.) " You have put on the new man, that is being renewed unto knowledge after the image of him that created him." (Col. 3:10.) The spontaneity of man is not eliminated through the grace in Jesus Christ, but it first rightly comes into its own. In relation to the grace of God, man is not tree or stone, but responding subject, responsible person; and faith, as certainly as it is God's gift, is man's original decision. For it is true faith, as the Old and New Testaments reiterate, only when it is " faith of the heart," that is, when the whole person affirms this faith with his words, but especially with his actions.

There is hardly another concept in the New Testament usage that is so appropriate as that of the *imago Dei* for expressing what is meant by the relation of personal correspondence:

God the Giver, in sovereign freedom, face-to-face with man; man, who responds with derived freedom, face-to-face with God;

God's " yes " to man — to man who as sinner lives in contradiction to God; man's " yes " to God, which is called into being by God's " yes " — is called into being but is not forced, remaining always man's own decision;

God's Word from which responsibility stems — which as Word of grace first really makes responsible; man's responsible decision, which God calls for and awaits, and which he at the same time gives;

149

the love of God that without setting any conditions turns itself toward man — man in whom no condition for merit is fulfilled — the love, however, which, just because of its unconditional nature, awakens trust in man, so that he takes the risk of laying himself completely and without reserve into the hand of this loving God, being conquered by this love; man who henceforth is so conquered by God's love that he returns God's love in reciprocal love;

this is what the New Testament seeks to express in the idea of the image of God in man.

10. The Doctrine of Sin

In this connection we can briefly sum up the Biblical *doctrine of sin*. The Old, as the New, Testament recognizes no other concept of sin than the understanding of it as man's self-chosen alienation from God, the Creator and Giver of all life. In this concept of sin the face-to-face relation between God and man consequently is expressed with particular penetration. Sin presupposes, on the one hand, that originally and inextricably the human being is *God's* human being, that he is not only created by God but indissolubly bound to God, be it in life or death, in salvation or disaster, in love or in anger; on the other hand, that man is genuinely God's counterpart, endowed by God with the power of free decision and therefore fully responsible for what he does, especially for his alienation from God. The connection between the two sides of this concept must be pointed out more exactly.

Even in sin man remains bound to God. He is always sinner *before* God; he sins always against God, with reference to God. Sin is always opposition to God, disobedience to him to whom we belong. It is rebellion. Sin is always an actual relation to God — that is to say a negative one, a perverted relation to God. Sin is indeed ungodliness — not in the sense that man is free from God, but that he would like to be free from him. The parable of the wicked husbandmen depicts this ungodliness

150

with incomparable clarity. Tenants they are and tenants they remain, even if they play themselves off as lords a thousand times and refuse to pay the rent. And, indeed, fundamentally they know that they are only tenants, not lords, but they do not want to admit it. They turn away from God in order that they need not see him; they kill his messengers, but in so doing they nevertheless have a bad conscience. Precisely for that reason they kill his messengers, because they have a bad conscience. But it is decidedly true that through sin the image of God in the heart of man becomes a caricature. "Although they knew God, they glorified him not as God, neither gave thanks; but became vain in their reasonings." Idolatry is the resultant of two components: the God-given knowledge about God and human sin, hence, a knowledge about God and yet no recognition of God. Recognition of God, one can have only in faith and obedience, not in sin. But wherever man turns himself to God he realizes, "Against Thee only have I sinned." How could man sin against God if he did not stand in an indissoluble relation to Him, if he knew nothing of Him?

As man remains bound to God even in sin, so sin is also the proof of his God-bestowed power to make decisions for himself. Nowhere in the Bible is God made responsible for sin. Even the strongest emphasis upon the omnipotence of God has its delimitation at this point which is never overstepped. It is not as if God did not have power over sin: he *himself* reserves this sphere of freedom for man; he himself, after all, in the creation of man in his own image made him a free counterpart of himself — man who can defy him, who can rebel against him. The treachery of Judas is no doubt a means in the hand of the redemptive God; indeed, the treachery of Judas is even an element in his eternal plan of salvation; but at this point, where human logic would like to go farther and draw the conclusion — that consequently God himself is the actual originator of evil, the real perpetrator — it stops and says no. Never! Man alone is responsible for evil, man carries the full responsibility for sin; he received from God as part of his freedom the power to sin, but the misuse of this power is entirely his own act.

151

Just as little use is made in the New Testament of the idea of the power of sin and of the universal hold of sin on humanity, in the sense that thus in some way, as the judges say, the single individual is less accountable for his sin. The power of sin is indeed a superior force, one that dominates all mankind; but this superior power of sin is man's own fault. Nor can the idea of the devil and of the evil powers of the unseen world be used to lessen man's responsibility. Nowhere is man represented as the innocent or pitiable victim overpowered by an evil superior force through no fault of his own, as occurs in the Greek tragedies. Not sympathy, but the severity of judgment and redeeming compassion are the lot of sinful man.

That man is thus held fully accountable for sin is a decisive proof of the inviolable nature of the basic Biblical idea that man is actually and genuinely, not only apparently, God's free counterpart. Sin is indeed itself slavery, and to be sunk in sin is to be incapable of good. But this is the consequence of sin, not its cause. Even while each human being is seen in his immediate relation to God, he is also seen as one who is jointly responsible for the entire history of sin. If he is the slave of sin now, he himself is to blame for his condition.

The sinful state never becomes the explanatory and accordingly excusable cause of the sinful act; for the sinful state is itself act. Even the idea of slavery to sin cannot therefore be allowed to conceal that of freedom of decision and the concomitant responsibility. Freedom of decision and inability to decide now for the good are two sides of one and the same human reality, the one turned toward creation, the other toward eternal death. And both are presuppositions for the Biblical doctrine of redemption.

V

The Biblical Understanding
of Truth and Doctrine (Continued)

1. WHY CHRIST?

THE CHRISTIAN FAITH, most simply expressed, is *faith in Jesus
Christ*. The church would have done well if it had always
withdrawn from involved doctrinal controversies to this simple
confession of faith, the only one which is explicitly contained in
the New Testament: Jesus Christ the Lord, Jesus Christ the
Son of God, the Redeemer. For in this simple confession the
nature of the Christian faith appears with complete clarity — it
is trust in and obedience to the personally present Lord. Faith
is not primarily faith in something true — not even in the truth
" that " Jesus is the Son of God; but it is primarily trust in and
obedience to this Lord and Redeemer himself, and on the
ground of this trust, fellowship with him according to his Word:
" Behold I am with you to the end of the world." Fellowship
with the living Lord who is present with us: this is what faith
in Christ in the New Testament preeminently means.

It is precisely this formulation which gives rise to the question: Why Christ after all? Why not simply God? How can we
understand faith in a mediator as the expression of personal
correspondence? Here, too, we can confidently expect to get a
twofold elucidation of our thesis as well as of the New Testament testimony about Christ, because our thesis itself was
obtained by using this testimony as starting point for our inquiry. To say that Jesus Christ is the content of faith, of truth,
is a radical departure from the ordinary conception of truth.
This is expressed in a decisive passage in the New Testament
itself; in the Prologue to the Gospel of John we read: " But

153

grace and truth came into being through Jesus Christ." Truth came into being! For one schooled in the Greek conception of truth this phrase is utterly perverse. Truth, after all, is precisely that which is timeless, the eternal which is not subject to change. For truth to *come into being* is a contradiction in terms. But truth that has come into being is the very core of the Biblical message. Truth is something that *happens*, that God *does*. Truth and grace can be spoken with the same breath: truth like grace is encounter between God and man; grace and truth came into being in Jesus Christ.

The presupposition of this tenet follows in the Prologue of the Fourth Gospel: " No man has seen God at any time." God, apart from his revelation in the form of a human being, is mystery. What we speculate about God is idolatrous interpretation of the divine mystery, of which we are all aware. The personal God can be known only in his personal revelation, and his personal revelation is the incarnation of the Word. The incarnation of the eternal Son of God is the unveiling of his quality of being person and hence at the same time his will to fellowship. For this is the Biblical conception of God's quality of being Person: love, self-communication — that love which through all eternity the Father has for the Son, and the Son for the Father. God's quality of being Person, revealed in Jesus Christ, is itself of such a nature that it establishes fellowship. Being person [*Person-sein*] and being in fellowship [*In-Gemein-schaft-sein*] are identical. Such is the Biblical concept of the personality of God. The revelation of himself as Person is therefore at the same time revelation of himself as Love; consequently truth and grace are the same. Not only are truth and grace manifested in Jesus Christ, but in him their real intentionality comes to realization. Jesus Christ not only reveals, he at once fulfills and realizes the will of God. Hence, " we saw in him the *doxa Theou*, the *gloria Dei*, the majesty of God." The incarnation of the Son is not only redemptive fact, but at the same time the realization of the divine world plan, the *oikonomia*, that is to say, the divine realization of the eternal purpose to comprehend the universe in Christ as

154

its head. We may not divide the nature from the will of God, as if they somehow were separable. His will is his nature; and his nature, his will. Hence, we may not talk about God without at the same time talking about his will, and what is meant by his will can be briefly stated: the Kingdom of God, revealed and grounded in the incarnate Son. The incarnation is not only our Lord's taking the form of a servant because of sin: at the same time it is majesty, because it is the realization of the divine world plan. It is the concretion of God's will to have a counterpart in whom his nature and his love are reflected and answer him. In Jesus Christ, God reveals himself as the God who approaches man, the God who because his nature is love wills that man answer him in love — in that love which he himself as Creator and Redeemer gives him. The event of the incarnation marks the coming into existence of truth and grace.

2. The Work of the Redeemer

Nevertheless, I believe that the ancient Christian development of dogma did not quite remain on the track of the Biblical revelation. The incarnation as such is not the pivotal point of the Biblical revelation, but rather the *work* of the Redeemer. Jesus Christ did not come merely to come, but he came to redeem. To be sure, only the incarnate Lord — very God, very man — can be the Redeemer. But the Bible guides us to ponder less the secret of the person of Jesus than the mystery of his work. Let me reiterate once more that apparent commonplace: not the substantive but the verb is the chief word in Biblical language. The old Christian theology converted the Biblical verb-theology into a Greek substantive-theology. That is the Platonic, substantialist element in it. The Bible is never substantialist, but always actualistic. It is essentially historical; but the contemplation of the natures of Christ misleads to a certain naturalism.

I must correct at this point certain emphases in my own book *The Mediator*. It was indubitably an unconditional necessity for the church to defend the unity of God and man in Jesus Christ

155

against all mythological, Gnostic, and moralistic-rationalistic attacks. But the church bogged (so to say) at that point. It gave the Christian faith a false orientation about the being instead of the work of Christ. In this way it imperiled the fundamental historical character of the evangelical message by means of a static Platonism. The Person of the Mediator must also be understood as an *act* of God, namely, as his coming to us in revelation and redemption. It must be understood as the divine act of turning himself toward and giving himself to man. In this sense Melanchthon's famous word, " To know his acts of kindness is to know Christ," signifies a decisive return to the Biblical understanding of Christ. We should compare with this statement the main Christological passages in the Pauline letters and we shall find it confirmed that predominant in the Biblical message is the movement, the coming down, the sending of the Son to us, his self-giving for us, his taking on himself the form of a servant, his taking on himself the sinful flesh, above all, his suffering, dying, and rising again, his obeying, his loving and revealing, his expiating and redeeming. Even the Person of the Mediator is comprehended with the verb, if I may so express it, not with the substantive. One could actually say: Jesus Christ, even and especially in his divine-human *being* as Person, is God's *act*, just as he is the *Word* of God. In him — not only through him — does God *do* something to us. In him, God reveals himself; in him, God reconciles the world unto himself; in him, God redeems us. Consequently, in this connection too, where we are considering the Person — the mystery of the Person of Christ — what is essential is not something as it is in itself [*Ansichseiendes*], a divine-human Person as he is himself [*Person-an-sich*], but the relation of God, the dealing of God with the sinful and lost humanity, the revelatory and redemptive *act* of God.

3. THE NAME OF CHRIST

Perhaps we can understand this whole point of view best if we begin by discussing the *name of Christ* itself. The Mediator has a functional name — the Messiah, through whom God rules and who carries into effect God's will to Lordship. Think of the parable of the wicked husbandmen, which I have already mentioned in another connection: the disobedient tenants who have usurped the seignorial rights are to be led back to obedience by the messengers of the lord. Finally he sends his own son with the same intention. The son is no messenger: he is the will of the lord himself, personally present. In him the lord stretches out his hands toward the property that has been wrested from him. Jesus Christ as the Messiah is restorer of the Lordship of God, the Kingship of God. *The office*, his function, gives him his name; God comes to us in his Son, in order to realize his Kingdom. Correspondingly, the first Christian creed apart from the Messianic name is the confession: He is the Lord. *Kyrios Christos*. In this Person the will to Lordship and the lordly power of God meet us. Jesus is the personified and incarnate kingly will of God; God's kingly will becomes a human person. To believe in him thus means primarily that one bows to his sovereign will as God's will and becomes obedient to him.

This becomes especially clear in the Johannine concept: Jesus is *the Word of God*. What God says to us is this Person. In him, God speaks to us his will, his intention, his decree, his world plan, his love. Unlike the prophets, he is not the conveyer of a word, a message — the prophet, after all, is nothing himself; not he, but his message is important. He himself is the message, his Person is God's revelatory doing. He himself, *in persona*, is the self-communication of God; consequently, we must always grasp the being and doing, the acts, words, and passion of the Lord as a totality. He himself therefore is the meeting with God (so to say); or, as the Old Testament believers expressed it, he himself is God's visitation to men, God's coming near, God coming to us, Immanuel. In him, God opens to us the mystery of himself. " Who sees me, sees the Father." He is the Father made visible — obviously not to the corporeal eye, but to the eye of faith. God's words were already given through the prophets; but these words were detached from the speaker himself. The prophets, if asked about the speaker himself

157

had to point away from themselves to the distant God. Hence, all prophecy is still unfulfilled revelation of God. What is lacking is unity between what is said and the presence of the speaker. Precisely this thought is expressed in the sentence: He himself is God's Word. When questions are now put about the One speaking, about the authority standing behind the Word, he no longer needs to point to the far-distant God, but may say: "But I say unto you, Come unto me." God's Lordship, previously only near to man, in Him is made directly accessible.

4. THE PRIESTLY OFFICE OF CHRIST

The third "office" of Christ, according to traditional interpretation based on Scripture, is the priestly office. Again the entire emphasis is upon the doing and giving of God. To clarify the idea that Jesus Christ is God's act of atonement, the Old Testament idea of sacrifice is used. It is a two-sided happening, an active and a passive — the priest sacrifices and the lamb is sacrificed. The New Testament says of Jesus: He is both priest and lamb at the same time, the One sacrificing and the One sacrificed. For he sacrifices himself. As in the Messianic title God's will to Lordship is meant above all else, so here God's will to fellowship. The concern is about "the office creating the atonement," by means of which what has been estranged shall be reconciled. That which divides is sin with respect to man, the wrath of God with respect to God. But it is never said that God is reconciled but, rather, that God gives himself in his Son for the reconciliation of the world unto himself. Even in the suffering of Christ, God is the active and giving, never the receiving, part. God receives nothing that reconciles him — not even a sacrifice agreeable to him; such an interpretation of the atonement cannot claim Biblical support. But God himself gives himself in the Son; the suffering of Christ is the act of God, namely, his giving, his giving of himself, by which he establishes fellowship.

We said at the start that in love, in the self-communication of God to mankind, God's will to Lordship, his self-realization, comes to fulfillment, Similarly, we can and must say that the entire revelation and realization of the divine will reaches its culmination in this giving of himself in Christ. For in this way God establishes fellowship, and fellowship is his real goal. In his self-giving to mankind in the cross of Christ, God reveals to us not only the most profound mystery of his heart — his love, his compassion — but he also creates that which is his cardinal concern, namely, fellowship, even while he gets rid of that which divides, namely, sin. The Person of the Mediator may never be understood apart from what he does in his suffering: " Behold the Lamb of God, who taketh away the sins of the world." The happening on the cross is the happening in which fellowship is established, the establishment of the " new covenant in his blood." Here the truth that God wills to reveal to us happens, a truth that he wills not only to reveal to us but also to *make actual* as fellowship and grace.

On this event in its concrete uniqueness, this Good Friday event (seen in the light of the subsequent Easter) — this " accidental historical fact," as Lessing called it — depends everything that we have said about the fundamental Biblical category: personal correspondence. Indeed, everything in the Bible is seen with reference to this basic category and bears testimony to it. But its essential meaning — the radical nature of this relation (the unconditioned *will* to Lordship and *will* to fellowship) and also the radical nature of the act establishing the relation — is fulfilled only in this unique event, and hence is understandable only with respect to it. We are dealing here with God's relation to mankind, a relation that is God's acting in space and time and therefore action in history. God's relation to the world and to mankind is not something timeless, but it is action in history. Its historicity is as unconditional as the relation itself: hence, this event is unique; it happened " once for all." Its uniqueness is as essential to this Good Friday event as the unconditioned will to Lordship and fellowship of that love which is disclosed in this unique event.

159

5. The Two-sided Nature of Fellowship

But we should quite destroy the whole meaning of our thesis if we were to stop at this point. For our thesis states that correspondence is demanded, that the will of God is fulfilled only when man's answer in response to God's Word has been given. For this reason the Bible never speaks of the objective event " Christ " by itself, but always at the same time of responding faith. " For God so loved the world, that he gave his only-begotten Son, *that whosoever believeth in him shall not perish.*" " But the righteousness of God is revealed without the help of the law, namely *the righteousness through faith for all believers.*" It is not as if this response, this answer to the word of God, were something secondary and additional — as someone has said, " a thousand meters lower " than that which God has done in Jesus Christ; but faith is spoken of on precisely the same level as Jesus Christ — so much so that Paul uses the two expressions " righteousness of God " and " righteousness of faith " interchangeably. If this faith is not reached, that also has not happened for which Jesus Christ came and suffered: the atonement, the fellowship between God and man. For this reason, he whose responsibility it is to preach atonement in Christ must appeal with all possible urgency: " Be *ye* reconciled! " The effects of the current are in evidence only when the circuit is closed. Fellowship, then, is a two-sided happening; the " yes " of man is precisely as necessary as the " yes " of God. Without faith there is no atonement and no redemption. If one counts the passages in the New Testament that speak of faith or in a similar sense of repentance, conversion, love to God, turning toward God, and what otherwise expresses the response of man, one recognizes how the meaning and truth of everything depends upon both sides and their correspondence. In fact one can say: *Faith is the truth.* For what God wills is that his name be hallowed, that his love find reciprocal love in man. To this end he gave his Son, that this could happen, *that by means of his self-giving, man would be led to self-surrender.*

6. The Preaching of Repentance

This refers first to the surrender of the sinful will which is estranged from God and in opposition to his will. God does not will the death of the sinner, we are told, but that he be converted. *Conversion* is first of all turning away from and repulsion of what is inimical to God, throwing away and negating the negative. Man must stop on the way he is going and must turn around. Everything depends upon whether or not this happens. The preaching of repentance is therefore the first task. With it the gospel of Jesus Christ begins, not only in the preaching of repentance by John the Baptist but also by Jesus himself. " Repent, for the Kingdom of Heaven is at hand." In repentance and conversion we find especially what we called before the divine conditional: " If ye are converted," " If the ungodly is converted," " If he turns himself toward the Lord "; or, in another grammatical form: " But he who is converted," " But he who believes," " Who repents," and so forth. The unreadiness to repent inevitably brings upon itself the wrath of God. Indeed, the divine grace itself becomes judgment where it is not met with readiness to repent.

With the concept of repentance or conversion the same radical change occurred in the New Testament as with all other concepts, and in this Paul also is pioneer. As in the grace of God not only a word is given by him but he himself gives himself in the Son, so the corresponding repentance can mean not only a change of disposition but man's surrender of himself. " Ye are baptized into the death of Christ and hence also through baptism into his death are buried with him." As on God's side a death is involved, so is it also on the side of man. The old man must die, he must be put off, he must be annihilated. And, indeed, man must of himself enter into this death. But while depicting this personal correspondence, Paul protects it from a serious misunderstanding. We have said that this correspondence is not equal on both sides. God is always first and the giver; man always second, the one receiving. In the same way the death that *we* die is Christ's death; in *his* death we are baptized, in *his* dying we are included. He himself draws us into his death. To die with him is therefore the work of grace; it is not man's own work.

But this does not mean an occurrence in which man is merely involuntary and passive. Man must go to this death himself, and with his whole self. He himself must consent to what happens to him; indeed, it takes place only by means of his consent. God's gift is of such a nature that it must become actual in a voluntary act of man, in obedience and trust. Man cannot do this of himself, but only when gripped by the love of God and the holiness of God, expressed in Jesus' death. But he must *himself* agree with the act of being gripped and reconciled. To be gripped is at the same time to grip: repentance is at the same time an act of faith. It must therefore be an honest penitence, a genuine repentance. God wants a free and wholehearted " yes," and in this " yes " a " no " that surrenders the whole man to God, that separates the whole man from sin. " So ye should consider yourselves as those who are dead to sin, but live for God in Christ Jesus." The whole person must surrender himself; hence, the expression " death " is the right word. Repentance means that I accept the death of Jesus Christ as a divine judgment upon myself and understand God's sentence of death, consummated in him, as being vicarious, and therefore a sentence that really should fall on me — and yet at once exempts me. In the sixth chapter of Romans, Paul develops the concept of repentance in its final, most radical form: the death of man corresponds to the death of Christ; the death of Christ must occur in order that this necessary death of man can also take place; the death of Christ is the actual stimulus in this happening to man, and yet at the same time it must happen as man's own decision; he himself must consent to this death.

7. The Biblical Understanding of Faith

While he is consenting to this death, he renounces what separated him from God, and he therefore participates in the life of God which in Jesus Christ the risen Lord is given to him as a

Presence. This is *faith* in the essential, positive meaning of the word, just as repentance is faith in a negative sense. Faith is resurrection with Christ to a new life. Faith, therefore, is not merely "believing something," but faith is a real happening that grips the whole person: coming into fellowship with the Redeemer, a genuine participation in his resurrection life. Faith means to be born again to a new life, to walk in the Spirit, to become implanted in Christ, to become a member of his body. Faith is, therefore, a genuine alteration of the person; indeed, a transformation of the person. Faith is the same as rebirth. The New Testament thus has made the concept of faith a radical one. As repentance is the death of the person who has deserted God, so faith is becoming a new person. In the Old Testament it is still called a new heart; but in the New Testament, a new man. Only that faith counts which is a new birth. We also see on the human side of the relation of correspondence how radically the conception of truth is changed. Even as the personal Word, the Son, took the place of abstract truth, so becoming a new person has taken the place of knowledge of truth.

And, indeed, this new being is one in fellowship or, therefore, a being in love, i.e., in the love of Christ. This, in turn, means participation in that mysterious being which goes from the everlasting Father to the everlasting Son through the Holy Spirit. What is of moment here is not union but fellowship. Subject and object may become one in a highest act of knowledge. The mystical experience of identification lies in the direction of knowledge, but it does not lie in the direction of faith. Faith should eventuate, not in union, but in fellowship. Fellowship is not, as abstract thinking always supposes, a form of union as yet unfulfilled. Fellowship is much more than — indeed, something quite different from — union. Union, in the last analysis, is being alone and living for oneself, but fellowship is being with another and living for him. The highest expression of fellowship in faith therefore means: to live for the Lord, to be instrument, to be servant — and yet at the same time to be child and son.

This Biblical understanding of faith, which is tantamount to what has been said about personal correspondence, stands in sharp contrast to the popular conception of faith. The latter is the product of the orthodox-objectivistic confusion of Word of God and doctrine. From the middle of the second century the church has instructed its believers that one " must believe " this and that doctrine in order to be a Christian — " whoever wishes to be saved must, above all things, embrace the Catholic faith." Once let dogma be the object of faith, and faith is then determined by means of the object-subject antithesis, by means of the rational concept of truth, and remains thus, even though the dogma is applied as revealed truth. Nor is this circumstance changed in the least if for dogma the word of the Bible is used as " revealed truth." Fundamentally, Bible-orthodoxy is precisely the same as dogma-orthodoxy, involving the application of the general concept of truth to revelation, instead of surmounting this understanding of truth by means of revelation. Where this confusion once dominates the understanding of truth, all subsequent instruction that faith is not only holding something as true but is " also " trust and obedience is futile. It comes too late; the damage is already done: from being a fellowship of disciples the church has become a school.

This misunderstanding of faith is noticeable in the fact that what in the Bible is meant as expression and description of the nature of faith has come to be understood as the object of faith. The Bible means that he who stands in faith is a new creature; the misunderstanding is, that we must believe that one becomes a new creature through faith. The Scriptures say that he who stands in genuine faith *has* the Holy Spirit and experiences the Spirit's living, renewing action; the misunderstanding is that one must *believe that* through faith he receives the Holy Spirit and that the Spirit is an animating, renewing power. The apostles speak of the ecclesia as the community and fellowship of believers, a community that can be experienced and that realizes itself in the exchange of gifts; the misunderstanding considers the church as the *object* of faith and even emphasizes that the *communio sanctorum* is not a fact of experience. The Bible speaks about faith being the same as being in reality allied to Christ; the misunderstanding replaces the real alliance by the alliance with Christ as *object* of faith, as a truth to be believed. This confusion, this replacing of personal understanding of faith by the intellectual, is probably the most fatal occurrence within the entire history of the church. It has been the cause of the too rapid expansion of Christianity and ecclesiasticism, which has so heavily encumbered the testimony about the revelation of salvation in Jesus Christ, and has lessened respect for the church more than anything else. For this basic ecclesiastical evil is the hidden cause of all others. Even the Reformation was not so free from this confusion of God's Word and doctrine that it could have completely freed the church from it, although the Reformers came close to overcoming it in their understanding of justifying faith.

8. Justification and Sanctification

But it was precisely here, on the central theme of the renewal of man in faith, as we saw in the third chapter, that very early the objectivistic displacement occurred. The purely transcendent or forensic comprehension of *justification* is cause as well as effect of the confusion between the personal and the intellectual concept of faith. For orthodox faith, justification is something to believe, a truth pronounced by God himself, a judicial sentence that at once absolves me and imparts to me the righteousness of Christ, a correct transaction before God's court of justice. What for Paul was a parable alongside other parables — i.e., the depiction of the divine transaction of judgment — in this context is taken literally by orthodoxy and understood as being conceptually adequate. In this way that " something," which for Paul only pointed to the merciful God himself who establishes fellowship with me, becomes the chief matter, the object of faith. Faith seizes this something offered by God, this absolution and impartation of the righteousness of Christ, as a " good " proffered by God; it has to do with this truth, not with God himself; this is faith in the dogma of justification as uttered

165

by God himself. That the doctrine of the mystical union and of sanctification *follows* immediately cannot repair the damage already done. This elaboration into a scheme of salvation, into a series of different phases of a process, only indicates that one is trying to join together again what in the New Testament is a unity, after it has first been separated. The division of this unity into three phases — justification, union, sanctification — is the attempt to counterfeit within the concept of truth determined by the object-subject antithesis what really lies outside its ken, namely, genuine personal encounter that establishes fellowship.

In the Pauline proclamation "justification, union, and sanctification" are one and the same seen from different sides, not a series of phases. In Christ, God himself lays his hand on me; he opens himself to me and opens myself to himself; he breaks through to me through the wall of my selfish I-isolation. He establishes fellowship with me and thereby at once becomes my Lord. That Christ is my righteousness is the same as that Christ is my life; the righteousness of God is no other than the righteousness of faith, and the righteousness of faith is simply the new obedience. That I turn from self to Christ is itself already the new life; that through faith I participate in the love of God which is in Christ is already the love of God poured out in my heart through the Holy Spirit. Nowhere in this context does faith depend on a "something" — not even on the "something" of justification — but only on Christ himself; for this reason Paul can pass from the "juridical" to the "mystical" formulation in the very same sentence: "Through the law I am dead to the law that I might live unto God. I am crucified with Christ; I live, and yet no longer I, but Christ, liveth in me." Who would attempt in this context to separate justification, union, and sanctification? Who would say which is first, which second, which third? In Christ as he is apprehended by faith, all is contained — justification, union, and the new life as life for Christ, instead of life for oneself.

When one stops dead with doctrine — even though it be divine doctrine — and does not advance to the reality signified "in, with, and under" the doctrine, it is only consistent that one distinctly places sanctification, the new life as life in love, "over against" justification as the "essential object of faith," as something that is not only second but also secondary.

In orthodoxy, quite contrariwise to the New Testament, there is much more and much more forcible talk about faith than about love. Correctness of belief is indeed the hallmark of this whole understanding of the gospel. If only your support of doctrine is clear and unequivocal, you are a Christian — however you may have disposed of the matter of love. That "faith" means to live for Christ as you trust Christ is forgotten; one now allows himself to relativize in such a measure the attainment of the new life in Chirst that even the dead "letter-faith" is considered valid as faith. The last step in this direction was reserved for the most recent times: the doctrine of the invisibility of the fruits of the Spirit.

In the New Testament it is true that the root is hidden — the life with Christ in faith — but not what grows out of this root, the new life; the sap but not the fruit. For to believe "in" the new life has no value, since faith is *itself* the new life. This new life is not something to be believed in but is itself experience of faith in Christ, who is present in the Word. The fruits of faith or of the Spirit are therefore precisely the tokens of faith becoming visible. By comparison with them one can determine whether one really stands in living faith or whether faith is only a matter of the head, a purely intellectual matter, a faith in the dimension of "believing something true." Whenever one knows of no other except this faith there is nothing to say about the fruits of faith — for this intellectual faith yields no fruit. In this way the fruits of faith are changed from being a *demonstration* of faith to an *object* of faith, and therewith the opportunity is also lost to test the genuineness of faith. It is further consistent, if this testing of the genuineness of faith, which is continually recommended by the apostles, is suspected as something contradictory to the essence of faith. How could it be otherwise when one has made of a demonstration and sign of faith an object of faith? This intellectualistic transformation of the concept of faith robs the church of the possibility of recognizing its poverty of faith by means of its lack of the fruits of faith.

9. The Church as Correlate to the Word of God

While we were speaking of faith and of the believer we elaborated an abstraction, which was necessary in the interest of clarity but which must now be resolved. This faith or this believer does not exist in itself or in himself. When the Bible speaks of the new life it speaks of life *in the community*, of life in the body whose head is Christ. Here, too, we shall have the task of settling misunderstandings that are determined through the false conception of truth, through the object-subject antithesis. We are dealing here with a misunderstanding of the church that is eighteen hundred years old. When the man in the street today hears about the church — be he Catholic or Protestant or what not — he thinks of an institution, a something that similarly to the state (even though in a different way) hovers over the individual, which has its own law and its own importance; a something that men use for specific purposes or that they serve with a particular aim; a something impersonal that, however, has significance for persons and their lives, and so forth. This concept of the church as institution roots in an objectivistic thinking that had already begun in the early days of the church and finally led to the complete transformation of what in the New Testament is called *ecclesia*. To state this from the start in an entirely clear, unmistakable way: *The New Testament knows nothing of a church as institution.* In the New Testament " church " means only one thing: the people of God, the community of the holy, the elected, the gathering of believers, believers gathered together. Not even the slightest abstraction has any part in what the apostles called church. Church is a concept understood purely and without exception as *personal*. Church is never anything else than the persons who through Christ, through fellowship with the living Lord, are themselves bound together into a living fellowship.

The Reformers again gave this New Testament idea of the church to the world, in which for centuries it had been obscured by an entirely differently conditioned, sacral-institutional concept and, above all, through a strange ecclesiastical actuality. But their knowledge had the power to succeed only in a very partial degree; the old institutional concept of the church, after Luther had seen through it and fought it with the greatest clarity and energy as error, forced its way back even into the Protestant Church, and the loophole through which it slipped back was the differentiating of visible and invisible church. The New Testament community in a certain sense no doubt also differentiated between the visible and invisible church — in the sense that even among the true members of the body there were also here and there false members, that is, those who belonged not genuinely but only apparently to the body of Christ. But with the church as institution this differentiation has not the least to do. The attempt is made to justify the institutional understanding of the church by appealing to its offices and sacraments, and to the Word of God given to the church. This is entirely incorrect. To be sure, the community has offices and sacraments and must have them necessarily; but they *are* not the church, any more than I myself *am* an instrument that I have and use — even though it be an instrument of the utmost importance to life itself and given to me by God. The church *has* offices, it *uses* sacraments; it therefore *has* institutions — if one wishes to place offices and sacraments into this category — but it *is* no institution. The church also has its rules and needs them; but the church *is* no set of rules, and the rules of the church do not constitute the church. In the New Testament the church is never anything else than the community of those who belong to Christ through faith, whom through his Word and Spirit he has constituted the community.

The church is therefore a magnitude to be understood as completely personal; it is the genuine correlate to the Word of God, which Jesus Christ himself is. The New Testament expresses this by means of the simile of body and members, of head and body: wherever Jesus Christ lives among men as Lord, as their Lord, there is the church. Consequently, the creation of the church and nothing else is of moment in this age. It is more correct to say that what is of moment is the creation of the church as the creation of faith or of believers, because the fel-

169

lowship-establishing Word and work of Jesus corresponds to the actual fellowship and not to the individual person or his faith. Jesus wills to hold man, the person — and he holds him through his Word in faith. But Jesus wills to hold man in fellowship, and again he holds him through his Word and the Spirit. Faith is nothing other than to become a member in the body of Christ. While the individual is released from his I-isolation, out of the sin that estranges him from God and man, he is taken into fellowship with God and at the same time with man. And, contrariwise, he will not be released in any other way from his I-isolation, except as he is taken into the concrete fellowship. The Word of God does not move aimlessly; even as the Word became flesh in Jesus of Nazareth, so it wills to work further as historical Word carried in man, as the faith-awakening witness-word of those who pass on to others what they have received. It is only by means of such a witness-word from other men that faith can come into being in any man. Through the incarnation of the Word, God himself bound himself to the historical Word, in order therewith also to bind us to this historical Word and in him to our fellows. As God himself enters history in his Son, so man is to be incorporated into the historical fellowship of believers.

The relation between the Word of God and the church is thus again that of personal correspondence. Paul once pointed this out with the simile of marriage. As the man gives himself to the woman and the woman to the man in human-natural love, so Christ gives himself to the community and the community to Christ in divine love. But again this correspondence does not signify equality. The relation of Christ to the community is quite different from the converse. Christ here too is inexchangeably the first, the One giving, creating, originating; the community is the established, the receiving, the created part. Christ is the Lord, the head, from whom comes all life and all guidance; the community is the body, which receives its life and direction from the head. And yet it is not simply the product of the head, as in the cause-effect scheme something is the product of something else. Between the community and Christ obtains a relation *sui generis*; namely, that of trusting obedience and of responding love, even as this same relation obtains among the members, that one serve the other in love. It is thus in the church that the consummate goal of God shines forth: the *Kingdom of God*, in which God's love is all in all.

10. THE NEW LIFE

And yet it only shines forth and is not yet present. The new life, the life from God, is not only promised, and to be believed in because it is promised. *This* eschatological interpretation of faith is again connected with the false objectivistic concept of faith and its falsely understood doctrine of justification. The New Testament makes clear that the new life is already present, just as certainly as that Jesus, the living Lord, dwells in us and that the Holy Spirit is given us as a pledge. It never says that we believe only in the promise of something that is future; rather, it declares that *in* faith we already *have* a real participation in what is future, in what is coming. But the consummation of what is coming is yet unrealized. For this reason, faith of necessity becomes *hope*. The church and faith are designed to further God's eternal goal of salvation and consummation, for this goal of salvation and consummation is the content of the divine revelation.

In the Christian community the new life is a divinely achieved reality, is indeed the action of God, himself present. But it is not yet what is solely real and what is solely efficacious. The body is still " the body of sin," not only in the physical but also in the social sense of the word. We yet live as a fellowship of believers in a sinful and perverse world. Sin is yet active within ourselves, and though conquered by means of the Spirit which dwells in us, is ever again sallying forth from its skulking place, from the " body of sin," into our life. Faith is assuredly the new life, but it is the new life struggling with the old. Consequently, faith is not itself ultimate. Faith itself is waiting as hope for another, the real ultimate, the vision, when we shall see God face-to-face and shall know even as we are known, when we shall be like him.

11. The Pledge of the Spirit

The Bible never describes eternal life, but tells us plainly what its essential nature is. It is the *gloria Dei*, and that means the perfect reflection of the divine holiness and the divine love in the creature — a creature who in order to be able to respond so fully to God's will must be newly created. For sinful corruption has penetrated to the very marrow of existence, but the earthly incompleteness as such is also a hindrance to attaining the final consummation. It is well expressed, " Who believes in me, he has eternal life "; he " will live, even though he die." But eternal life cannot develop in a mortal body, the holy Will cannot fulfill itself in an actual person who is partly given to sin. The new life that we receive in faith is, after all, the life of the risen Christ: therefore, what has already been received, the Holy Spirit dwelling within us, is only the " first stroke "; it is only the " pledge " of the resurrection life which fulfills itself. " If the Spirit of him who awakened Jesus from the dead lives in you, so he who awakened Christ from the dead will also make your mortal bodies immortal by means of his Spirit who lives in you." The new is present but only in germ, upon the development of which through a new act of God we can only wait. But we can wait in certainty. For it is one and the same Spirit that dwells in us and that will awaken us.

12. Consummation

The goal from the point of view of the individual is "to be like him "; from the point of view of the community it is the Kingdom of God. The simile that the Bible uses for the latter is the meal — the convivial meal, the feast, or the wedding banquet — or the " face-to-face vision." In both ways of expression the same is meant: direct intercourse with God and through him with one another. By means of this direct intercourse, however, we become as John says, " like him." The image of God, after which we are created, will then be consummated in us. God will thus effect his perfect Lordship and his perfect self-

172

communication, and at the same time man will be perfected in that for which he is created and determined. The relation of personal correspondence is then fulfilled; truth is then realized as the perfect Presence of God with his creation and the perfect presence of the created with the Creator through him who is the eternal Word and who through all eternity is destined for incarnation. For " if Christ, our life, will be revealed, then ye too will be revealed with him in glory." If then not union but fellowship, which is rooted in God's self-communication, is truth, then this is the last word to be said, as it has been said.

VI

The Biblical Understanding
of Truth and the Church

To some extent we are now in a position to understand according to its origin and to weigh according to its meaning the antithesis of objectivism and subjectivism from which we started in the first chapter. Objectivism is determined by the correct observation that in the creation of His connection with man God's act is first. The Creator is prior to and independent of his creation. The Word of God is prior to and independent of faith; God's act of atonement is prior to justifying faith; the call of the church and its sacraments is prior to the faith of the individual; the Bible is prior to the inspiration of the Holy Spirit. As the eternal Son takes human nature upon himself in Jesus of Nazareth, not the contrary, so God's free action is always first and creative, man's answer is second and what is created.

All this, objectivism would maintain and place on a firm footing. Consequently, what may be called the substance of the church is always to some extent preserved with it, however great the damage may be that it causes. At any rate in Catholic sacramentalism the sacrament was perpetuated, in its clericalism the church, in its dogmatism the Word of revelation — in some way these were always perpetuated, even if in a markedly distorted form, as in the legalism of Pharisaism something of the holy will of God was always safeguarded. Subjectivism is doubtless the genuine church dissolving tendency, which more seriously jeopardized the welfare of the revelation, even though as reaction it has often had a certain beneficial effect and even

174

though it was often in the form under which Biblical truth would blossom out against torpidity. Its relative power, if one would briefly express it, is the observation of the fact that God's free rule of the Spirit can be received by man only in an equally free spiritual act. Subjectivism, therefore, holds to the second basic fact of the relation of personal correspondence. Because or insofar as it isolates it from the basic fact, it has no substance of its own, but it lives, so to say, by virtue of its opponent, objectivism, as a protest movement. But to designate it as Protestantism for this reason, as happens time and time again, and therewith to understand the Reformation as an apparent form of this subjectivism is (as we now know) to miss the point completely. Not every protest movement is Protestantism — and we should notice in addition that the very name Protestantism for the Reformation has an apocryphal origin and questionable value. As objectivism leads to torpidity, so subjectivism to dissolution. What is torpid can be awakened again to life; but what is dissolved is no longer in existence.

1. THE NECESSITY FOR THE DISCUSSION WITH OBJECTIVISM

If in spite of what we have just said we wish critically to analyze only objectivism in this lecture, we do so because the struggle against legalism is the real struggle of the church. Objectivism has always been the real ecclesiastical danger within the church — through all centuries and even now. From within the church its danger is much more difficult to recognize, and the struggle against it was always the most dangerous. For the opponent will feel himself attacked in his most sacred precinct and will consider himself called to be guardian on the battlefield of the holy treasure entrusted by God to the church. Within the church the struggle against false ecclesiasticism and false orthodoxy in all times has been most necessary and most difficult. But we may not forget for a moment that even as we are now contending against one side, we also have the opponent on the other side in every era.

But we will not concern ourselves with ecclesiastical objectiv-

175

ism in general, but with those of its appearances with which we ourselves have to deal in our own situation, namely, within the churches of the Reformation and their theology. I should like to consider especially three such forms: objectivism in doctrine; objectivism in office; objectivism in the sacrament.

2. The Doctrine of the Divine Infallibility of the Text of Scripture

We have already dealt with *objectivism in doctrine*, that is, with orthodoxy, in detail and in review. We have yet to recognize several of the apparent results. *Objectivism in doctrine* consists in equating or failing to distinguish between God's Word and doctrine. In the lands of the Reformation this false identification is made chiefly with relation to Holy Scripture. The mistake is not that orthodoxy called the Bible, the entire Holy Scriptures, the Word of God, rather, that in its tendency toward security it legalistically misunderstood this Bible-as-God's-Word in the sense of something disposable. The doctrine of the divine infallibility of the text of Scripture is a clear parallel to the doctrine of the infallibility of the pope. The difficulties and corruption that developed therefrom in the church are known. With this doctrine the church got upon the path of a theological Docetism. As with the ancient Docetists the human nature of Christ was appearance, so in this connection the human nature through which the Word of God enters into the Bible was considered appearance. The word of Luther, that the Bible is the crib in which Christ lies, was not understood in all its profundity. Genuine Bible faith — because the Scripture is the cradle — self-evidently belongs together with Biblical criticism; for a Bible free from error would no longer be human, and, contrariwise, the recognition of the humanity of the Scriptures calls for a distinction between the fallible vessel and its divine infallible content. Through orthodoxy, however, Biblical criticism as such is excluded and its application is abhorred as a sign of unbelief. The history of the disintegration of this orthodox view of doctrine is not without a certain tragic aspect.

176

How much genuine Bible faith was spoiled or hindered or compromised through a false theory of the Bible! The Word of God could surely call out to the church, " For your sake my name is calumniated among all peoples." For the fact that so many modern folk wish to have nothing more to do with the Bible, this false seeking for security must carry not a little of the blame. But this is all well known.

3. THE HISTORY OF SALVATION BECOMES THE DOCTRINE OF SALVATION

Another misunderstanding connected with the first is less well known. By means of the identification of Word of God and doctrine, a specific ecclesiastical doctrinal system quite apart from verbal inspiration — mayhap the Lutheran or the Reformed doctrine — was equated with the Word of God in the Holy Scriptures. One simply disregarded the fact that the Bible gives us the Word of God in a multiplicity of doctrines in part very different and even contradictory. The Pauline theology is not the same as the Johannine or the Synoptic, the New Testament theology is not the same as the Old, and the Priestly theology in the Old Testament is not the same as the prophetic. Whoever gives the Bible a chance to disclose its genuine meaning knows this, but classical orthodoxy dare not admit it. It must therefore either ignore these differences in doctrine or explain them away through the use of allegorical interpretation. Genuine Bible faith intends to hear from the Scriptures the single, never contradictory Word of God, but it is free enough to recognize that this one Word manifests itself in very various doctrines: it does not identify Word of God and doctrine. But orthodoxy does not recognize this distinction; paradoxically, it therefore actually falsifies the Scriptures which it intended to protect. That God can speak to us his single, never contradictory Word through the priestly writings of the Old Testament as well as through the prophetic or the New Testament writings, even though these several writings are very various and in part contradictory, just as he can speak his single, never contradictory Word through the contradictory accounts of Luke and Matthew in regard to this or that incident in the life of Jesus — this correct proposition was converted into the following false one: There are no contradictions in the Bible, either in statements or in doctrine; all such contradictions are only apparent, and can be resolved by means of the harmonizing or allegorizing interpretation. The hidden Docetism also becomes manifest in this connection. One does not believe in the genuine historicity of the divine revelation. One does not take seriously that actually in the Old Testament the fullness of knowledge was not yet present, the knowledge granted to us in the Word becoming flesh in Jesus Christ. The historical revelation is converted into a timeless system of truth. Wherever allegorizing is done, either the Platonic concept of truth or the Judaic legalism is always operative. The *history* of salvation is converted into a timeless *doctrine* of salvation.

4. What Is Meant by " Proclamation "?

A further consequence that necessarily follows from the basic error of orthodoxy is the overvaluation of doctrine in the life of the church and in the faith of the individual. The church has received a holy vocation to teach because of the indissoluble sacramental connection between doctrine and Word of God. But the primary commission of the church is not doctrine but proclamation. Proclamation, I suppose, must always have a doctrinal content, but it is itself something other than doctrine. It is faith-awakening, faith-furthering, faith-wooing address. Genuine proclamation always has a prophetic character — even if we preachers are no prophets; pure doctrine, on the other hand, has a didactic character. There is a kind of " proclamation " which is much more suitable for the Jewish synagogue than for the Christian church, even though its doctrinal content is New Testament. The confusion of doctrine and Word of God gives to theology and to theological doctrinal disputes an altogether disproportionate importance. Not enough stress can be placed in the congregation upon doctrine and knowledge of

178

doctrine; but the measure of doctrinal development that the individual and congregation can endure without suffering injury to their faith is always proportionate to the measure of practical realization of that faith. A congregation in which much living prayer and much hearty brotherly love is present can digest much doctrine; doctrine will nurture it in faith, in love, and in hope. But when faith has little strength practically to shape life, an overdose of doctrine is really deadly. In this connection the church, with its orthodox attitude, perpetrated egregious pedagogical errors, from the consequences of which it yet suffers. But whenever the proclamation itself is confused with doctrine, the Pauline assertion — " faith comes out of proclamation " — becomes poisonous. The church then believes that it need only pile doctrine upon doctrine, without troubling about practical results and without noticing that in this way it kills souls instead of awakening them to a true life. It is high time that the church again thought through its practice of preaching and instruction in the light of the knowledge that the traditional identification of doctrine and proclamation is a destructive error. The mistakes that follow from this basic error of orthodoxy are not corrected by constantly alleging that the Word alone is efficacious. Of course the Word alone is efficacious, but doctrine is not — not even Biblical or catechetical doctrine. When we consider the Biblical understanding of proclamation, we observe that it means an event entirely personal, in the nature of a personal meeting, which is far different from the catechetical homiletical traffic in dogma that is determined by the Greek concept of truth.

What we ordinarily understand and employ as sermon and instruction is foreign to the Bible itself. The *missionary* proclamation of the apostles has only a distant relationship to what takes place in our preaching, and whether there was in the already existing congregation something analogous to our sermon is at least highly questionable in view of the portrayal in I Cor., ch. 14. This is not said to discredit the sermon as in the course of church history it has become the form of proclamation, but rather to point out that this teaching nature of proc-

179

lamation is linked with certain historical presuppositions; that, therefore, this kind of proclamation is not " the " proclamation, but rather is one of many possible methods of proclamation, the particular serviceableness of which must be proved anew by the church in every generation. The same obtains for " instruction." Here more numerous critical voices from within the church itself are stressing the need for reflection about whether our traditional regulations for instruction are really ordained by God. The notion that instruction, hence the mediation of doctrine, is the best means to lead young people to faith is in any event difficult to verify in the Bible, and it does not seem that churchly practice has in any way furnished proof that it is. The general complaint about the pedagogical scandal of our customary instruction is too widespread for one to fail to hear it.

Once let the relation between Word of God and doctrine be rightly understood, and there will hardly be room any longer for the view that the single thing which the church could do for the awakening of faith is the conceptual clarification of the Holy Scriptures. Has it, then, not yet been noticed that the most perfect knowledge of Biblical concepts and the entire acceptance of Biblical doctrine is wholly compatible with the completest want of actual faith — and indeed that this is anything but a rare phenomenon? Need one always fail to notice that " to speak the Word of God more distinctly " has very little to do with a yet more thorough theological indoctrination? The notion that the completest catechetical instruction, be it for adults or youth, is the best *way* to faith is the product of an undue stress upon logic — even though supernatural — which has very little to do with what the Bible itself calls " proclaiming the Word of God." It is much rather a consequence of that confusion between the two concepts of truth of which we have been speaking. The practice of the ancient church as well as that of modern foreign missions and of evangelization seems to us to point another way: that the actual function of doctrine — the doctrinal sermon as well as instruction — normally belongs where there is already a confessional congregation, where the concern is no longer with establishing a believing congregation, but rather with strengthening faith and deepening knowledge of faith. But the proclamation that seeks to initiate faith is a form of the Word in human speech that is vastly different from the doctrinal presentation. This the church must learn from those who have achieved results worthy of emulation in the missionary and evangelistic fields. But the church will first be able to learn it when it has discerned as error the false identification of doctrine and Word of God. This is one consequence of our theological reflection, perhaps the weightiest and most practical.

5. The Sacrament of Baptism

The second question, *Objectivism in the understanding of the sacraments,* leads us directly into actual and critical ecclesiastical problems. I must confine myself here to the sacrament of Baptism. The old controversial question of whether the New Testament says anything about child Baptism will not be raised now. Whether or no it does, the fact still remains that in those passages where Baptism is spoken of didactically, where its significance is shown for faith and the church, it takes place in this way, that the fact of Baptism is a two-sided happening which conforms completely to what we have called personal correspondence. In Baptism it is God, first and sovereign, who acts, who forgives sin, who cleanses man and regenerates him. But man too acts in Baptism. He allows this cleansing of himself to take place, he lets himself be drawn into the death of Christ, he confesses his faith and his attachment to Christ. Baptism is not merely a gift to man, but also an active receiving and confession on the part of man. Indeed, Baptism, precisely as this free confession of man, is the stipulation for the individual's joining the church. Baptism is not only an act of grace, but just as much an act of confession stemming from the act of grace.

In the Catholic doctrine and practice this sacrament became entirely separated from its original Biblical meaning. Baptism is an *opus operatum,* man is *object* of the divine act, grace is

181

applied to him in a way that takes no account of the fact that the one being baptized is a subject; in certain exigencies unborn children are also baptized in the womb. Child Baptism — more precisely infant Baptism — really becomes normal and what is taken for granted.

The Reformation retained infant Baptism for understandable ecclesiastical reasons. It found therein a particularly powerful testimony indicative of the anticipatory grace of God, on free election grounded purely in the goodness of God and not in man's disposition or circumstances. But in that way it encountered dogmatic and practical difficulties which heavily encumber Reformation churches to this day. The principal proposition of the Reformation in the doctrine of the sacrament, which brought to sharp expression the opposite of the Catholic *opus operatum*, was *nullum sacramentum sine fide*, the inseparable intimate connection between sacrament and faith. To be sure, faith does not produce the sacrament; but the sacrament is not accomplished, it is no true sacrament, without faith. Luther and his successors drew from this basic proposition the necessary conclusions for infant Baptism. Grant that infant Baptism is a genuine sacrament, that there is no uncertainty about it, and we admit that infants too have faith. Orthodox Lutherans assure us that the faith of the infant, inasmuch as it is genuine faith, lacks neither the knowledge of the Word nor assent or trust. Even Calvin defended this interpretation, though somewhat faintheartedly; but he certainly moved another idea into the foreground in accordance with the precedent of Zwingli: the idea of the covenant. It is not so much the individual faith of the infant as, above all, the faith of the " household " by means of which the baptized infant is qualified to be accepted into the covenant of God. But both the Lutheran and Reformed trends of thought have their difficulties. In the first place, the concept of faith becomes unclear — for what does faith mean if we attribute knowledge, assent, and trust to an infant who otherwise is incapable of understanding or consent? But in the second place covenant and body of Christ are separated. For even if by virtue of being a member of a Christian

182

household one can in some way be reckoned as being in the covenant of God, yet he can certainly not be considered as belonging to the body of Christ, to which none belongs except believers. Altogether devious is a new interpretation of the sacrament of Baptism, in which in any event no question is asked about faith, whereby the speaking of the words of promise suffice for the sacrament as such. With this interpretation — in contrast to the classical Lutheran and Reformed one — personal correspondence is given up and the sacrament is equated with the missionary sermon.

Neither the Lutheran nor the Reformed Church found its settlement of the question of Baptism entirely satisfactory. It was noticed that the New Testament declaration of Baptism could be linked neither with the idea of infant faith nor with that of covenant faith by proxy of the parents and witnesses in their firm conviction [plērophoria]. Something in the relation of personal correspondence was disturbed, and this feeling led to the introduction of confirmation, which could not be Biblically grounded. In confirmation the missing factor of response in the New Testament Baptism act was recovered (so to say): the personal " yes " as man's answer to God's promise of grace. The whole of the New Testament act of Baptism was thus divided into two parts: the objective gift of grace in infant Baptism and the subjective confession of faith in confirmation. Although by and by confirmation was introduced practically everywhere, this settlement too never particularly pleased the church. The statements of the New Testament about Baptism continued to be connected with infant Baptism and yet the bad conscience roused by this identification was soothed by completing Baptism with confirmation, which certainly does not stem from the Bible.

This difficulty increased, the more frequent and crass the instances were where persons who had been baptized as infants and therefore were included in the covenant of God arrived at the power of making their own decisions and turned their backs on the church and the Christian faith. Most of the contemporary neopagans and also most members of atheistic societies have been baptized as infants; what does the grace of Baptism, of which in any event they probably never even heard, mean for them? What does the fact of having been baptized mean for the large number of contemporary people who do not know and do not even care to know whether they have been baptized? Infant Baptism, which has its good points in an entirely Christian fellowship — that is to say, a fellowship of persons who all joyfully profess Jesus Christ as their Lord — becomes a highly questionable arrangement where it is requested more from consideration of custom than from conviction of faith. It becomes a questionable arrangement when judged on the basis of the undervalued fundamental assertion of the Reformation: *Nullum sacramentum sine fide* — the sacrament is not valid without faith. In this Reformation principle the basic Biblical fact of personal correspondence is again expressed.

In the contemporary objectivist bent of theology the tendency is so prevalent to stress one-sidedly the objective element in Baptism that there is no longer even any awareness of the difficulty of which we have been speaking. What is of concern is not faith, it is said, but only the divine word of promise that is spoken over the infant. Where one separates the Word of God and faith to this extent, the character of the sacrament is destroyed, for the truth of the proposition *Nullum sacramentum sine fide* cannot be denied. The word of promise spoken over the infant is then nothing other than a *sermon-word*; none inquires about the efficacy of the Word. But the sacrament of the New Testament is not only a sermon-word, but a bifrontal happening in which God says "yes" to man and man says "yes" to God.

None knows better than the missionary that this is true. I do not know of any evangelical mission where infants are baptized without decision; much rather with infants as with adults who are to be baptized, the presuppositions of faith are inquired about, with the latter the individual himself being asked, with the former the "household." No children of unbelievers are baptized, only children of Christians; that is to say, one acts on the basis of the proposition: *Nullum sacramentum sine fide*.

184

This was also the presupposition of the Reformation practice of Baptism. All our ancient baptismal liturgies implicated as the essential element the confession of faith of the parents or the witnesses to the Baptism, and the vow to provide Christian instruction for the one being baptized. This means that infant Baptism will be undertaken only when, according to human measurements on the basis of the confession of faith, the proxy-faith of the persons responsible, the "household," can be regarded as present. The demand for confession of faith and responsibility for Christian instruction at that time led to no important conflicts, because, disregarding exceptions, everyone was ready to acknowledge the creed of the church, and instruction was obligatory. With the cessation of these historical conditions the presupposition also dropped away under which alone child Baptism could be justified on the basis of the Bible — although this too, as we saw, was not without certain difficulties. The contemporary practice of infant Baptism can hardly be regarded as being anything short of scandalous.

6. Visible and Invisible Church

This question of Baptism of children is not a single question in the large complex of church problems but, rather, is decisive for the entire churchly practice, since Baptism is the basis for church membership. He who has been baptized in the Lutheran or Reformed congregation belongs to the Lutheran or Reformed Church. The host of correctly baptized persons who inwardly or outwardly have been completely alienated from the church must therefore be reckoned as belonging to the church. The church, after all, in the course of the centuries, has utilized the objective factor so one-sidedly as criterion of itself — correct doctrine and right administration of the sacrament — that for long it has lacked the means or will to remove from its membership baptized persons who at heart are completely alienated from it. Objectivism in the concepts of sacrament and church led to an expansion altogether too rapid, which immediately must become manifest in directly tragic measures as soon as on

185

is obliged to use personal criteria for church membership; that is to say, therefore, as soon as anything like a personal confession is encouraged. Then the comparatively little group of believers separates itself from the mass of millions of baptized unbelievers or those uninterested in the church. The church, up to this time a fiction, becomes a fact.

By appealing to the difference between visible and invisible church one may not legitimize theologically (so to speak) the people's Church of Constantine, to which everyone belonged and which had over against it no nonchurchly world. This justification of existing conditions, stemming from Augustine, overlooks two factors: first, that this differentiation between visible and invisible church is also necessary in the purest confessional church; and, secondly, that it may not be placed in opposition to the demand for the confessional church. He who does not want to confess Christ does not belong in the church. The church can hardly separate with certainty genuine from spurious faith — God alone can do that, and therefore the true church is invisible — but it can and should determine who intends to confess Christ and who does not. The relinquishment of this requirement of confession — indeed, the relinquishment of any confessional criterion — and the sufferance of manifest atheists in the church is a relinquishment of an essential mark of the church. Church discipline must never be obscured by an appeal to the necessary distinction between visible and invisible church, which is of quite another dimension. The surrender of this essential characteristic is attended with a prodigiously serious displacement: the displacement of the concept of the church from the personal to the institutional. Count among church members such as openly do not confess Christ, and the church can no longer be considered a community of believers, but only as an institution, an instrument for the development of the believing community. Perhaps this displacement was a practical necessity, perhaps this "people's church" is still today something worth retaining, but then it must be made clear, and clearly taught, that by church is understood something totally different from the church of the New Testament and that this difference has nothing to do with the differentiation between visible and invisible church. The " church " as institution is not the " visible " one, and the church in the personal sense is not the " invisible " one.

7 THE COMMUNIO SANCTORUM

We should also never forget that this too rapid expansion of the church in large measure began with Constantine. For that is but to say that it stands in a reciprocal relation to the objectivistic concepts of sacrament and church of the early Catholic Church. One-sided objectivism at all odds is a distinctive characteristic of the Catholic Church. The church is understood not so much as *communio sanctorum* as holy institution, sacramental establishment of grace, and hierarchical legal organization. Not the Word, but the sacrament and the office, is decisive, and the sacrament as *opus operatum* of the rightly ordained bearer of the priestly office is independent of faith. In the Reformation the contradistinction between this sacramental-ecclesiastical objectivism and the New Testament testimony about faith and church was recognized and asserted. Luther never wearied of reiterating in his era that the church is nothing other than the *communio sanctorum*, the group of believing Christians. The confessional congregation undoubtedly stemmed from the logical conclusion of the Lutheran concept of the church — a conclusion that Calvin in his way drew by requiring public confession of the individual. But reasons arising from concern for the people's welfare argued for the preservation of the people's church inherited from the time of Constantine. It was perpetuated by means of infant Baptism, which really meant infant Baptism commanded by public authorities and protected by penal sanctions: Woe to him to whom it should occur not to bring forward within the shortest possible time his newborn child for Baptism! The compulsion fell away, but the custom remained after faith and the inner connection with the church of Christ had long since disappeared. The discrepancy between these two churches, the gigantic church of those

187

baptized and the tiny church of those assenting to confession, is one of the chief causes of the present difficulties of the church in all places. Seen in the long church-historical perspective, the essence of the situation in which the present-day church finds itself is above all the replacing of the people's Church of Constantine by the pre-Constantinian church of those making confession. If the church again is a community of those who confess Christ, personal correspondence, despoiled by objectivism, is again restored. The meaning of the church as living in fellowship, confessing the Lord, can again become distinct. The fatal inheritance from Constantine is liquidated, and with it the false objectivism in the understanding of the church.

The right content in the idea of the people's church, grounded in consideration for the developmental nature of faith, should in this way not be denied. The advance of the confessional church easily leads to an individualism that is just as foreign to the New Testament church as the institutional idea of the church. Even if an infant and some adults, who indeed grew up in a Christian home but who have not really been gripped by the Word of God, cannot in the genuine sense be counted in the community of Christ, yet in a sense they belong in some way within the province of the church so long as they do not directly in a negative decision dissociate themselves from it. This is what was really meant in the Reformed doctrine of Baptism, with its reference to the Old Testament idea of the covenant, and this is what was retained as its token in child Baptism in spite of all its dogmatic difficulties. This trend of thought certainly does not destroy the personalistic idea of the church, but, on the contrary, builds upon it, yet gives it (with regard to the developmental nature of faith) a less rigorous interpretation in which this tendency reckons with a confession yet latent (so to speak), a preliminary form of genuine decisive faith. Account must however be taken of the fact that the use which can be made of this less rigorous thought of the covenant must be restricted by the degree to which the church finds itself in the missionary situation, and to the extent that it does not live in the midst of a people who profess the Christian faith, but rather finds itself a minority among a people who are indifferent or hostile to the church.

The third question can hardly be separated from the one just discussed, namely, objectivism in the understanding of the office. The Protestant ecclesiastical office is much more strongly encumbered than is ordinarily granted with an ancient Catholic tradition of office that deviates from the New Testament. The circumstances are known through which in the second and third centuries the priest-bishop office developed. The New Testament recognizes no difference between clergy and laity, between a " spiritual " profession and a nonspiritual people of the church. All are spiritual who are joined with Christ in faith through the Holy Spirit. As such they are also all active, not only in daily living but in the worship service of the congregation. Setting over against each other active-expending and passive-receiving parts of the church is, as the fourteenth chapter of First Corinthians shows, unknown to the New Testament community. This unbiblical procedure is the correlate to the ancient Catholic, unbiblical concepts of bishop and priest.

8. The New Testament Understanding of Office and the Reformation

The New Testament, to be sure, knows " offices " in abundant differentiation and gradation: apostles, prophets, evangelists, teachers, the episcopate, the diaconate, elders. But entirely disregarding this fact, that the multiplicity and kind of these offices do not remotely correspond with those of the Reformation Church, they are also distinguished from those of the later church by the fact that they are wholly spiritual and nowhere determined by ecclesiastical law. The offices stand in a specific correlation to *charismata* and for that reason the efficacy of the office-bearer was definitely linked with his *charisma*, his divine endowment. Only at the end of the New Testament epoch, in a period about which we know through the post-Pauline pastoral epistles, the beginning of a canonical interpretation can be faintly traced. Not only in this regard, but in regard to various

189

other criteria, it can be noticed that we stand at the border of ancient Catholicism. In this period bordering the New Testament epoch it is not yet possible to discover that a bearer of an office simply on the strength of its once having been conferred on him should have a specific authority, irrespective of his spiritual qualification and testing, solely by virtue of the canonical act of ordination. This concept of office is incompatible with the spirit of the New Testament.

In this respect the Reformation, going back to origins, substantially corrected the Catholic development in the wrong direction. But it did not carry this development to its logical conclusion; on the contrary, it very soon turned back to the Catholic trend because of practical considerations and because of the transformation in the understanding of the church which set in early. The Reformation, to be sure, proclaimed the universal priesthood of all believers and fundamentally denied the difference between layman and religious; but it did not allow itself to draw the practical conclusion to this fundamental proposition: it hardly aspired toward reinstituting the general, active participation of members of the congregation in worship and the responsibility of all members for the functions of the body, not to speak of being able to put it into effect. The picture of the worshiping congregation in the Protestant Church, just as in the Catholic, is not as in Corinth the circle where each in succession made his contribution to the common edification, but actually what we understand by a church service of worship, that one who gives stands up before the crowd of those who receive. The Protestant Church became a " clergyman-church " [Pfarrerkirche], a congregation in which in substance one man is responsible for all that the congregation does, and the rest therefore remain more or less without active responsibility. The Reformed Church certainly corrected in a significant way this one-sidedness of the minister's church by means of the eldership and the diaconate, but it too failed to restore the original balance.

190

9. Mistaken Developments

From this unfulfilled reformation of the church, from this being bogged halfway between Catholicism and the New Testament church order a series of important conclusions can be drawn. The one man who faces the whole congregation as the solitary leader of worship is essentially a teacher and dispenser of the Sacrament. For only doctrine and administration of the Sacrament, not other spiritual functions, give rise to this setting of clergy and laity over against each other. The pastor justifies his sole responsibility for doctrine through his monopoly of theological training, his being set apart with a view to administering the Sacrament by means of his monopoly of canonical ordination. Both move in the direction of an ecclesiastical objectivism after the Catholic pattern. This objectivism comes to a clear expression above all in the acceptance of the anti-Donatist propositions in the Augsburg Confession.

On the basis of the Catholic idea of the church it is logical to explain that the dispensing of salvation is wholly independent from the person of the ecclesiastical giver, the bearer of the office. We are dealing after all with an *opus operatum*, with a magical-hyperphysical event. The canonical objectivism of the office and of the completely impersonal official action belongs to the material objectivism of the Sacrament, of the sacred substance of the Host. The Bible knows nothing of this objectivism. The Word of God in every age is certainly infinitely superior to the man to whom it is entrusted. By way of exception, God can surely even speak his Word through an unbeliever. But the proclamation is certainly always meant and enjoined to be a testimony of faith — "I believe, therefore I speak" — and a prophetic happening. Not the moral condition of the bearer of the office as such is constitutive for the delivery of the Word, but "anointing by the Spirit"; to be armed with the Holy Spirit — which no ordination as a canonical act is able to confer — is decisive for the power of the proclamation. Proclamation is an event of a personal character that moves "out of faith into faith." Only he can actually speak the Word who has himself been gripped by it and thereby has also been transformed. An unbeliever can expound pure doctrine, and lack of belief detracts in no way from the clarity and Biblical correctness of his doctrine. Doctrine is impersonal-objective, is separable from the person; prophetic proclamation of the Word on the contrary is not. Consequently the anti-Donatist formulas of the Augsburg Confession wholly fail to conform with the genuine Reformation concept of the Word of God and proclamation, but rather to the orthodox objectivization of the concepts of Word, faith, and proclamation. This objectivization, as an invincible residue of the objectivistic interpretation of the church, from the beginning kept pace with the reformation interpretation of the church, and to an increasing degree usurped the latter's place.

The presentation of pure doctrine requires no spiritual qualifications, but certainly theological study. One could very well be a skilled theologian who could make subtle distinctions between the concepts of pure and corrupt doctrine without having real, living faith. For the mediation of pure doctrine, therefore, a bearer of office who believes is not necessary, but only one who is theologically trained. So the strong emphasis shifts from spiritual-personal to impersonal-intellectual, from genuinely churchly to scholastic. The attempt is made to hide this deficiency of churchly qualification by means of canonical qualifications. Correctly to administer the Sacrament neither a particular amount of theological training nor a real " anointing by the Spirit" in the sense of personal faith is necessary, but solely the canonical ordination. One must be *rite vocatus*, lawfully called to his vocation.

Being called to an office in the New Testament — be it apostolic, prophetic, diaconate, or episcopate — is always a highly spiritual happening, an event that takes place between God and man through the Holy Spirit, at times with and at times without human mediation. Of a fixed, impersonal-canonical ordering of this relation there is no trace to be found in the New Testament. It is the sign of clerical transformation when canonical qualifications replace spiritual. Where the first question asked concerns the *rite vocatus* no question is raised about spiritual quality,

192

but simply about concurrence with ecclesiastical law. One must not allow himself to be deceived by the liturgical clothing and theological interpretation of the canonical act of ordination: by gradually transforming the spiritual-personal characteristics to those of the canonical order, the nature of the office becomes something quite other than it was in the New Testament.

10. THE ECCLESIASTICAL OFFICE AND CONTEMPORARY MAN

Two characteristic displacements in Protestantism concerning the office — that from the prophetic-personal Word of God to pure doctrine and that from spiritual to canonical qualification for the office — above all else make the ecclesiastical office questionable for contemporary man. Theological education is not able today to establish a unique ecclesiastical position, in a time when Bibles and education are accessible to everyone. The time when only the " reverend " gentleman was able to interpret the Bible is past, however great may be the benefit of a theological training in exposition of the Bible. According to the universal priesthood, in principle every member of the congregation is an independent Bible reader. At the time of the Reformers the practical realization of this principle was precluded by the many delimitations to the educated life. Today these hindrances for the most part have fallen away. The monopoly of position of the theologically educated in the congregation is weakened; the office of the Word must be reconstituted to conform with the New Testament meaning. But the office of administrator of the Sacrament has also outgrown its one-sided canonical basis and constituting; we again require of a priest who as representative governs a priestly congregation more than that he be *rite vocatus*, and can no longer reconcile the calling to office with canonical ordination.

To this we must add a second, positive factor. The general intellectual development of man in modern times has led to the situation that if a man becomes a Christian through God's grace, he can no longer understand being a Christian as merely a passive belonging to a congregation, but he must interpret it (at all odds in the New Testament meaning) as responsibility for the congregation. The contemporary Christian intends to share responsibility, intends to give his strength in the service of the church, and is disillusioned by the church if it withholds from him this right of service. A church that gives him nothing to do cannot satisfy him. The historical development thus leads the church back to the position that it was starting to give up at the beginning of the second century and to which even the Reformation was unable to lead it back: to the church that practically as well as fundamentally was the church of the universal priesthood of all believers, to the overcoming of the false objectivistic concept of the office, taken over from the Catholic Church. We cannot foresee in what way the renewing of the New Testament actuality of the congregation will accomplish itself in detail. But it is certain that such renewing will bring with it a basic transformation of the church and will have far-reaching consequences for its entire upbuilding and activity. The pastor — that is to say, the believing Christian who has the advantage over the others of a thorough theological training — will also have his necessary place in this newly formed church; but the time of the "clergyman-church" is definitely past.

11. The Pastoral Word

The day of the "clergyman-church" is past for the single reason that it is no longer able to meet the spiritual needs of our time. It is somewhat astonishing in what measure the apostles, who "turned the world upside down" with their message and whose word in an incomparable way had the character of a public proclamation to the whole world, dedicated themselves to pastoral work with the individual. "I never stopped," said Paul in taking leave of the Ephesians, "to admonish *each one of you with tears day and night.*" The most intense pastoral work directed to the individual by the man who proselytized half the world and established countless congregations! The contemporary pastor of a large city, and sometimes even more the pastor of a small city or large village, must feel ashamed in the face of the Pauline injunction, " Admonishing every one with tears." What can pastoral work mean in our congregations of four thousand souls and more! But the apostle Paul assures us throughout all the letters that public proclamation without personal pastoral work is not to be justified. Should this hold valid less today than in those times — today, with a people spoiled and conditioned by individualism and psychology, who no longer attend public preaching services and are no longer able to understand the Word to all as the Word to the individual?

Once again this is an objectivistic interpretation of the Word of God which has no understanding of the individual cure of souls. The presentation of doctrine does not necessarily require personal ministry to the individual. What is said to all can equally meet the need of the individual because of its conceptual clarity — logic and grammar are the same for all persons. Why should one say particularly to the individual what one has already said so plainly on Sunday to all together? Pastoral work is taken seriously only when one knows that delivering the Word of God is something other than presenting pure doctrine, that to the delivering of the divine Word belongs the will that this Word should take possession of man, should lead him " to the obedience of faith "; hence, when concern about the Word is also concern about its being impressed upon the individual and taking shape in him. Pastoral work is proclamation interpreted in love to the individual. Therefore in a quite particular degree and in a singular fashion it can be reduced to the quite personal event of proclamation of the Word of God which the Bible continually exhibits to us. Most of the discourses of Jesus are thus not general proclamation — " Let whoever will, hear " — but pastoral conversation. Similarly, the Word of God delivered by the prophet is frequently a message to an individual person. Nathan did not deliver a catechetical sermon to King David. By divine commission he spoke the Word of God to him as a highly personal pastoral word. The fundamental Biblical relation of personal correspondence between the Word of God

195

and the human answer becomes especially apparent in such pastoral care.

Thanks to its objectivistic tradition, our church is very poorly endowed for such pastoral care. Quite apart from the fact that the almost exclusively scholarly preparation for the ministerial office does not create the most favorable conditions for the pastoral activity, the number of pastors in contrast to the number of those who need the *cura specialis* — and according to Paul everyone needs just that! — is ridiculously small. The church, if it wishes to discharge its pastoral duties even in a measure, urgently needs lay workers. In pastoral service too the universal priesthood attains its highest realization, for here the individual spiritual experience and personal familiarity with the Bible is of much greater import than systematic theological studies, while the public interpretation of Scripture in the sermon demands special schooling. But, conversely, a sermon that grew in a context of such pastoral work by laymen would merit, as our present-day preaching does not, the title of preaching in the name of the congregation.

12. THE OBJECTIVIZED CHURCH

In conclusion, I should like to link together what we have now come to recognize in three aspects as false objectivism in the church with what was said earlier about the difference between personal and institutional church. Whenever the church is not understood primarily as fellowship, but as " establishment," as institution, as " something," it is objectivized in a false way. This objectivization occurred on the part of the Reformation Church because in the proclamation of the Word of God pure doctrine, and in the Sacrament the factor of administration in perfect form, was emphasized first and foremost, if not exclusively. This had already occurred in the early days of the Reformation through Melanchthon's linking the objective characteristics of the church, pure doctrine, and correct administration of the Sacrament, with the definition of the essence of the church in the Augsburg Confession. The question about the

196

characteristics of the true church is definitely legitimate and necessary; the New Testament time and again speaks of them. Yet it is certainly of little value to consider pure doctrine and correct administration of the sacrament as such characteristics; but — one thinks for example of the standards that the letters applied to the congregations — the quality of the daily life of the members, expressed in numerous ways, must prove whether God's living Word is present and efficacious in a congregation. But Melanchthon by the marks of a true church understood something quite different: objective criteria, ironclad, disposable standards. As such, pure doctrine and correct administration of the Sacrament offer themselves to him. In contrast to the living Word of God, both can be fixed, at least in a measure, once for all, and like a standard meter, a disposable measure, manipulated. From the correct proposition, "The true church is and becomes everywhere where the Word of God is livingly present," the false proposition was formulated: The true church can be discerned through the existence of right doctrine and the correct administration of the Sacrament. With this *quid pro quo* a second is linked: the concept " characteristic of the true church " is connected by means of a clarifying relative sentence so closely with the concept " essence of the church " that the misunderstanding was almost unavoidable, namely, that pure doctrine and correct administration of the Sacrament *constitute the essential concept of the church*. In this way the personal concept of the church — which is the only New Testament one — is obscured by the objectivist concept of institution; and the revolutionary perception of Luther — that the church is nothing other than a fellowship of persons, namely, the believers who through their present Lord, their head, are connected with a body — was again lost. In place of the two-sided concept of the church, which expresses personal correspondence — the church is the fellowship of believers that is grounded in God's Word — the one-sided objectivist concept entered: the church exists wherever pure doctrine is proclaimed. This proposition, altogether false, one can now trace as the principal proposition throughout the entire doctrine of the post-Reformation church.

— as if there were not also a proclamation of God's Word that did not immediately awaken faith and hence did not create a church. The false, one-sided objective concept of the church is certainly also to blame for the church's no longer understanding itself as a missionary church.

The reduction to two of the criteria for the true church given us in the New Testament, and indeed to the two that offer themselves most easily to objectivization, namely, pure doctrine and correct administration of the Sacrament, resulted in the period following in a tremendous impoverishment of the church. The New Testament provided standards for congregations to examine themselves with respect to their being genuine churches: whether they held fast to the Word, whether they were in obedience, whether their faith was alive, whether they were fruitful in the works of love, steadfast in bearing suffering, zealous in service for the Lord, joined together in true brotherly love and mutual admonition. While this personal correspondence of Word of God and obedience-in-faith is precisely the genuine object of self-testing, everything is now limited to the two objective criteria that characterize the church as institution but not as fellowship of faith. That the church turned so much toward doctrine, so little toward discipleship, is a chief reason for its weakness, which is now becoming apparent. A church that detaches itself from the world only in speaking, even if it were speaking in the purest Biblical doctrine, but not in action and love, becomes unworthy of belief to the world. It deserves such a condemnation as the Bible has already clearly pointed out. One-sided objectivism, since its beginning the genuine inner danger of the church, must work particularly destructively in the Church of the Reformation, which grew out of the struggle against this very objectivism.

We are at the end. It has proved fruitful to us, we hope, to explore the entire range of the church and its theology with the searchlight of the concepts of objectivism and subjectivism and so to test their understanding of Biblical truth. The right to do this we have taken from the Bible itself, in which all truth is understood as the truth of a relationship, namely, the relation of personal correspondence between the Word of God and human obedience-in-faith. With this concept of personal correspondence we did not compass any kind of rational principle, grounded in itself and understood by itself; but we comprehended that which forces itself upon the mind of the observant Bible reader as common denominator of all Biblical proclamation, which is indissolubly linked with the Biblical understanding of God and the Biblical history of revelation. That the Biblical understanding of truth is " historical " is an old notion. The meaning of this historicity we have tried to understand anew on the basis of the Bible itself as the truth that is superior to the object-subject antithesis and the rational concept of truth determined by it. The truth of which the Bible speaks is always a happening, and indeed the happening of the meeting between God and man, an act of God that must be received by an act of man. Doing the truth — this is the characteristic unphilosophical, non-Greek way in which the Bible speaks of truth. In the measure that this understanding of truth again becomes alive in it, the church will itself be renewed again into the true church. For this renascence we are hoping.

INDEX

I. Subjects

204

207

II. Names

Husserl, 15, 16, 48
Huxley, 33

Irenaeus, 29, 39
Isaiah, 137

Jansenius, 57
Jaspers, 16, 17, 49
John, 34, 42, 46, 172
John the Baptist, 161
Judas, 151

Kähler, 82
Kant, 13, 14, 19, 20, 28, 29, 39, 49, 111
Kepler, 11
Kierkegaard, 7, 16, 17, 18, 28, 42, 43, 44, 58, 59, 60, 84, 112

Lao-tse, 137
Leibniz, 11, 15, 57
Lessing, 159
Linnaeus, 10, 34
Locke, 58
Luther, 45, 47, 56, 61, 76, 78, 81, 126, 127, 134, 136, 142, 143, 147, 169, 176, 182, 187, 197

Marcel, 21, 49, 60
Medicus, 17
Melanchthon, 47, 66, 156, 196, 197
Moses, 52, 137

Nathan, 195
Newton, 11
Niebuhr, Reinhold, 59
Niebuhr, Richard, 59
Nietzsche, 57

Noah, 146
Nygren, 59

Origen, 48, 56

Paul, 26, 42, 46, 56, 74, 104 f., 114, 119, 120, 121, 122, 123, 124, 125, 126, 135, 145, 148, 149, 156, 160, 161, 162, 165, 166, 170, 194, 195, 196
Pascal, 13, 34, 52, 57, 58, 59, 60
Planck, 33
Plato, 7, 8, 49, 60
Plotinus, 49

Reymond, 59
Rickert, 14, 31
Ritschl, Albrecht, 79, 80
Ritter, 56
Royce, 59

Sartre, 16, 17, 49, 60
Schelling, 11, 59
Schlatter, 82
Schleiermacher, 3, 45, 52, 79, 80
Schneeberger, 47
Secrétan, 59
Socrates, 7, 8, 18, 111
Spinoza, 25, 49

Taylor, 59
Thévenaz, 59
Tillich, 59
Troeltsch, 81

Vinet, 58
Von Hügel, 59
Von Ranke, 56

Weizsäcker, 53
Windelband, 25

Zwingli, 67, 182

210